Rose Zwi, daughter of Jewish Lithuanian parents, was born in Mexico, lived in London and Israel, but spent most of her life in South Africa. She has lived in Australia since 1988. Author of five novels, she has won several prizes for her work, including the 1980 Olive Schreiner Award for *Another Year in Africa*, and the Australian Human Rights Award for Fiction in 1994, for her novel *Safe Houses*.

OTHER BOOKS BY ROSE ZWI

The Inverted Pyramid
Exiles
The Umbrella Tree
Safe Houses

ANOTHER YEAR
IN
AFRICA

Rose Zwi

Spinifex Press Pty Ltd
504 Queensberry Street
North Melbourne, Vic. 3051
Australia
spinifex@peg.apc.org

Published by Spinifex Press, 1995

Cover design by Lin Tobias
Made and printed in Australia by Australian Print Group

National Library of Australia
Cataloguing-in-Publication data:

Zwi, Rose.
    Another year in Africa.

    ISBN 1 875559 42 6.

    I. Title.

A823.3

*To my Mother and Father
who taught me how to sing,
And to Dina who listened.*

I

*B*erka Feldman spat out the nails from between his lips, cleared the table of leather, tacks and thread and left the shoe on the last, to be repaired the following morning. It was only ten to five. He seldom left the workshop before six, but today he felt restive. After an oppressively hot morning the sky had suddenly darkened and distant thunder had rolled like wagon wheels over rocky ground. Ripped by forked lightning the clouds emptied themselves over the suburb then drifted away, leaving a brilliant sunset and steaming streets.

From the doorway he watched the water gurgle down the gutters towards the Dip. He drew a deep breath. His lungs caught sharply on the smell of damp concrete and a sudden yearning for the wet-straw smell of the veld washed over him. He longed to be on his wagon again, enclosed in the silence and emptiness of the veld, with only his voorloper to lead the oxen. In summer he had watched the grass bend and sway like Jews at prayer while he hummed the half-forgotten songs and psalms of his childhood. In winter he listened to the susurrus of the wind through the dry grass, rising to a mournful swell as it swept over the veld. Towards evening a thin spiral of smoke might appear on the horizon. He savoured his solitude, certain that it would end. Soon he would walk into a mud-walled farmhouse filled with the smell of coffee and griddle cakes baking on an open fire. Hanging from the rafters of the reed-and-thatch roof would be cobs of dried mealies, twisted rolls of tobacco and strips of biltong. From the earthen floor into which peach pips had been beaten would rise the faint sweet smell of cowdung . . .

How free, how lonely that life had been.

He took off his leather apron, washed his hands in the cracked basin at the back of the shop and rinsed out his mouth. The taste of nails persisted. Only a drink would remove that metallic taste, but if he came home on a Friday evening smelling of beer, Yenta would have another weapon in her armoury of abuse. He put his cap over his thick grey hair and walked out of the shop, squinting up at the sun which hung low over Main Street.

From where he stood he could see the eastern part of the suburb; from the top of Main Street he would see the rest. The city lay to the east, its tall grey towers rosy in the dying light, a coppery blaze piercing the eye as the sun reflected off glass and steel.

To think that forty-five years ago it had been little more than a miners' village with row upon row of tin shanties, rough men, horses, ox wagons. Berka shrugged his shoulders at the miracle of its growth.

His shop was a mile and a half from town, but the Dip brought the buildings nearer and they towered like a fortified city over a village at its gates. Although he might yearn, occasionally, for his carefree days as an itinerant cobbler, he had lived in the shadow of the city for so long that he gladly accepted the boundaries of his world: The sun rose to the east of Main Street, and set over the hill, to the west of it.

Berka recalled clearly his arrival in South Africa, early in 1892.

'It's a bad time to have come,' his uncle reproached him. The pogrom should have coincided with a boom in South Africa. 'There's no gold in the streets nor, it seems, in the mines,' he continued crossly as he led Berka into a small room at the back of the Concession Store. 'You'll have to work hard. I pay five pounds a month with free board and lodging. If you want to get rich, save.'

For several years Berka sold blankets and trinkets to black miners. On week-ends he helped in the Kaffir Eating House attached to the store. The smell of burned entrails and cooked meat clung to his clothes and cleaved to his nostrils. His cousins sniffed fastidiously when he came to his uncle's house for an occasional meal.

In his sparsely furnished room he studied English from a tattered grammar book. The bar was his elocution class. From the English miners he acquired a Midlands accent which, coupled with impeccable Yiddish inflexions, made his teachers roar with good-natured laughter. He read voraciously. This improved his English, widened his knowledge and assuaged the loneliness of his years as a kafferitnik. He worked for long enough to buy the tools of the trade he had learned in the old country, then started on his life of wandering.

His uncle never forgave him his ingratitude.

'If you'd remained with me instead of running off into the veld like a wild chatas,' he said to Berka, 'you'd have been a rich man. Today you don't even own the house you live in.'

'Property is theft,' Berka had replied. 'I want nothing that I haven't earned with my own labour.'

They never spoke to one another again.

Berka stood at the corner of Main Street and Lovers' Lane. Wherever he looked he saw Uncle Feldman's possessions. He had become a man of property over the years. But Uncle Feldman was not a happy man; he had little joy from his sons. They had not gone beyond Standard Seven in school and proved equally inept in business. He would be lucky if they said a decent kaddish for him when he died — at a hundred and twenty years, please God. Berka chuckled. He could think of no greater punishment for his sons.

Uncle Feldman had moved out of Mayfontein twenty years ago but he retained his Concession Store, the source of all his wealth. He hired a manager and although he was almost eighty, he still went to the business. At irregular hours, Berka thought grimly, so that he could catch the manager stealing. Uncle Feldman was certain that everyone stole from him.

Berka spat into the gutter.

Uncle Feldman was one of the few people towards whom Berka could not extend tolerance, an attribute which he valued above most others. Yenta, who had never really understood him, claimed that his tolerance stopped at his own front door.

He began walking up Main Street, aware that his tall bulky figure was as much an institution in Mayfontein as the headgear of the mine, the white dumps on its outskirts or the bar. As he walked to and from work every day he was hailed from all sides.

9

His heart swelled with emotion: He was the friend of Jew and Gentile, the arbiter in disputes, the consoler in sorrow. In short, he was loved.

'Feldman!' came a deep voice from the smithy across the road. 'Why do you stand there in the middle of the street, smiting yourself on the chest, smiling, spitting, shaking your fist?'

Leib Schwartzman emerged from the smithy. He was a stocky man whose powerful shoulders gleamed with sweat under his grease-stained vest.

'Are you sick that you're shutting shop so early, or has your uncle written you into his will?' he asked with a grin.

'Neither. I calculated that if I worked an hour less today, I'd become a millionaire that much later. How's business?'

'Bad, bad.' Leib wiped his forehead with the back of his hand. 'Cars, trams, bicycles. Where have all the horses gone?'

'To the Free State, to become rabbis like that ass Benjamin,' Berka said.

'Don't blaspheme against the servants of the Lord. What will happen when you have to account to Him one day?'

'If God is just, as you claim he is, he'll distinguish between those with kosher stomachs and unkosher souls. I may not get to heaven but neither will my reverend brother-in-law Benjamin. The only trouble is that I'll probably meet him in the Other Place.'

Leib laughed. He had studied Law in Kovno but influenced by the workers' movement he had given up Torah for a trade. The future of society, after all, lay in the hands of the proletariat. But he had retained his love for Jewish tradition and went to shul, to synagogue, regularly. Opiate of the masses, he'd exclaim angrily when Berka defined religion for him. What's a worse opiate? Going to shul or going to the bar? Meet my learned friend Bernard, he would mock. He's so thirsty for Justice that he's been called to the Bar.

'When I saw you packing up early I thought perhaps you wanted to get to shul in time,' Leib smiled.

'Don't joke,' Berka said gloomily. 'I'll probably land up doing that to please Ruth. It's not easy being an honorary grand-father. Ruth's afraid I'll land up in Hell because she once heard me say that there was no God. She wants me to look for Him in shul.'

'Strange child,' Leib said rubbing a grease spot off his arm. 'Last week your sister-in-law sent Ruth to borrow a pot from us. "Mrs. Blackman," says Ruth to the wife because she's speaking English now so the name's Blackman not Schwartzman, "mine grenny vants to lend your big bleck pot." Why doesn't she speak Yiddish to my Chaya? They're both a pair of English scholars, Ruth and Chaya.'

'Because she doesn't know Chaya well and to strangers she speaks only English.' Berka looked angry, upset. 'I must be getting along. I'll stop off at the bar to chat with our local proletarians.'

Leib put his hand on Berka's shoulder.

'Don't be angry with me, Berka, I know how fond you are of the child. But to whom can one speak? To her father the dreamer? Or her mother who's always wrapped up in Vicks and cottonwool?'

'Ruth's not strange, Leib. She's got too much imagination and too few friends. The kids tease her because she doesn't speak English properly. She'll learn. She begins school on Monday where she'll mix with other children. Have a good sabbath. See you at the poker game on Sunday night.'

The sun had almost disappeared behind the Main Street hill and Berka stepped up his pace. He wanted to see it set behind the mine dumps. There were few sights he loved more.

Poor Ruthie. She'd have to learn to live in the present. A child of six burdened with a consciousness of tragedy and persecution, with memories that weren't even hers. He himself was guilty of telling the story of his family's massacre in her presence. He had broken down that time and shouted:

'There is no God!'

Berka coughed to clear the heaviness on his chest. He hummed tunelessly for a while then remembered the song about the drunkard:

> When they write my epitaph
> It'll read 'Here lies a drunk',
> And I'll answer with a laugh,
> 'There's no brandy here, I'm sunk!'

He must sing that for Yenta. She said that real Jews didn't booze. Yet here, immortalised in a Yiddish folk song, was the lament of a Jewish drunkard. Let her explain that one away. Berka walked on, humming the jaunty tune.

There were few people in Main Street. The Jewish house-wives were at home preparing the sabbath meal and the miners' wives shopped on Saturday morning. Haggard, often toothless, their hair perpetually in curlers, they trudged across the veld in their slippers from the mine's Married Quarters to do their weekly shopping. There was little enough in their purses after their men had stopped off at the bar and at the bucket shop on Friday evenings. Their children, thin and snot-nosed, ran wild through the suburb.

Harsh men, these miners, yet who could judge them? Here he was, walking in the clear rain-washed air while they were thousands of feet below surface, drilling into stubborn rock, breathing in poisonous fumes, stumbling through the tunnels that honeycombed the earth beneath his feet. Underground was Hell. Dark tunnels of damp rock, slippery passages, unbearable heat, pressure bursts, rock falls. Could these conditions produce gentle compassionate men? And what was it all for anyway? They wrested a few grains of gold from tons of rock, then buried it again in underground vaults.

He had watched the men come off shift, their faces pale with dust and fatigue, tin hats in one hand, carbide lamps in the other, blinking in the unaccustomed light of day. They washed down the mine dust with drink and beat up their wives, their children and the hapless mine kaffirs. To them, the blacks were barely human.

Every year Berka watched the black recruits arriving at Mayfontein Railway Station clad in loin cloths and blankets. They were tall sturdy men, selected for their strength and good health. For two shillings a day, a pot of mealie meal and kaffir beer, they travelled hundreds of miles from their kraals and their families to live in crowded mine compounds and to do the hardest work underground. When their nine months' contract ended, they might be a few pounds richer, wear trousers and a shirt, and carry away with them, under their gay blankets, a lung disease.

And the white miners organised unions to protect them-selves from the blacks' cheap labour, but left them to be slaves to the mine bosses.

'Berka! You look as though you're carrying the world on your shoulders,' a gentle voice said at his side. 'And all the way uphill too.'

'Reb Hershl! Just the man I need to see.' Berka stopped at the bakery door and sniffed. 'Ah, you perfume the suburb. There's such comfort in the smell of fresh bread. Little wonder I've got such a big nose. All my emotions are filtered through it.' He put his arm around Hershl's shoulders and walked into the bakery with him. He had time. There would be another sunset tomorrow evening. Such a pessimist he wasn't. A few words with Hershl would remove the metallic taste from his mouth and the ash from his soul.

Hershl took off his floury apron and hung it on a nail behind the counter. The bakery was small. The front portion had been divided off from the wall ovens at the back by a thin wooden partition. There was a glass-fronted counter which displayed iced cakes, buns and several kinds of bread: rye with aniseed, special sabbath kitkes and sandwich loaves. Through the opening in the partition came a surge of hot air as the iron doors of the wall ovens swung open to receive another load of bread. A loud crash of metal trays and bread tins drowned the first part of Hershl's sentence:

'. . . the last lot of loaves for the night,' he said as the noise died down. 'Dirk will lock up. Since I took him on I can go to the synagogue on Friday evenings.'

'How's business?' Berka asked.

'Excellent, improving all the time. It paid to take on a trained baker. Faigel works up front now and only does the confectionery for special occasions. I bought a horse and cart this week. The deliveries were getting too big for my bicycle.'

'Leib will be pleased to hear there's another horse in town,' Berka said. 'He thought they'd all gone to the Free State.'

'Free State?' Hershl looked puzzled. He did not always understand Berka's jokes. 'Did I tell you I'd made an offer for Sharp's delicatessen? It's much bigger than my shop and I can build in extra ovens. Now that I've got contracts with a few Concession stores I shall need it. I saw Uncle Feldman the other day,' Hershl added. 'For two reasons. To get an order for the bakery and to ask for a donation for the Refugees' Fund.'

'Let me guess,' Berka said drily. 'The order you got at cut

prices. And if you did get a donation, you had to sweat blood first.'

'You know the man. He denied he was stingy. All rumours, he said. People thought he was mean because he didn't advertise his charitable deeds as others did. He gave anonymously.'

'So anonymously that he doesn't even sign his cheques.' Berka retorted. 'Let's talk of cheerful things.'

'Cheerful things?' Hershl's face dropped. 'There's nothing cheerful in 1937. Look at Germany: Jews thrown out of jobs, property confiscated, schools closed, people shut up in ghettos. That's cheerful? And suddenly the world's too overcrowded to take in a few Jewish refugees.'

'They let some Jews into South Africa from Germany.'

'And are drafting the Aliens Act to keep the others out. They hate the Jews as much as the Nazis do.'

'But what's happening in Germany couldn't happen here,' Berka persisted.

'You've been saying that for years, Berka. This isn't the same South Africa you knew in the old days. All those stories you tell of Boer hospitality and respect for the people of the Book. When they're in the Book they're all right, but when the farmer's crops fail and he comes to borrow from the Jewish storekeeper at interest, it's a different matter. When the Jew was a smous, a pedlar, they tolerated him. When he holds the purse strings or he's in competition, they fear him. And where there's fear, there'll be persecution.'

'Nonsense. There may be hotheads among them but has there ever been a pogrom here?'

'What do you think the Greyshirts are planning, a Purim party?'

'So, where's it better?'

'Where's it better he asks,' Hershl appealed to the ceiling. 'Berka, we need a home of our own, without Aliens Acts and without anyone's kind permission to exist.'

'Spare me the Zionism. Bought any good stands in the sea lately?'

Hershl laughed, not without embarrassment. I shall die in Jerusalem, he predicted when he argued about Zionism with Berka. That I can believe, Berka would reply. To live there is

14

another matter. Emissaries from Palestine had an easy time with Hershl. Two years earlier an imposing man with a dark flowing beard and side curls had sold Hershl a stand in Palestine. A few months later he discovered it was situated a mile off the coast of Jaffa, in the sea.

'Nu, in Lithuania I was a Hebrew teacher,' Hershl said. 'Here I am a baker. In Palestine I'll become a fisherman. Remember how furious Faigel was? She doesn't understand how I feel about Palestine. Buying trees, making an annual contribution to Zionist funds, sending other people, that she doesn't mind. But the idea of settling there is beyond her comprehension.'

'And mine. It's too remote and strange to me. How's the family?'

'Fine. Daniel starts school on Monday.'

'So does Ruthie. It's a pity they don't play together. It'd help if Ruth had friends her own age.'

'Daniel's also shy. Children of immigrant parents have a hard time. Torn between different ways of life. If we lived in Palestine . . .'

'There he goes again,' Berka said walking towards the door. 'I live in the present and you live in an impossible dream of the future. It's better, I suppose, than living in the past like our Dovidke. Come here, Hershl. Look at him standing there at his window, dreaming of the old country no doubt, where the fields were greener and the fruit sweeter.'

'He often stands like that,' Hershl said looking up at Dovid Erlich at his workshop window over the road, gazing sightlessly into the distance. 'He's got problems. Not much work coming in, mostly alterations. And Sheinka is a nagging wife.'

'Is there another kind?' Berka asked.

'Poor Ruthie. She's caught in the middle. They can't be easy parents to live with. I wonder what went wrong? Sheinka was a lovely woman when they came out from Lithuania eight years ago. A little melancholic perhaps, but charming. She's grown bitter over the last few years.'

Berka was looking up at Dovid. From his first floor workshop, he thought enviously, he can see over the ridge of the hill where the sun will soon set. And he's not even aware of what he's seeing. Berka turned to leave the bakery.

15

'Have a good sabbath, Hershl. Come over and kibbitz on Sunday night. Leib and I have arranged a game of bloff. Low stakes.'

He shook Hershl's floury hand warmly. He loved the man; he renewed Berka's faith in humanity.

Main Street was shining after the rain. A tram car clambered heavily up the hill, packed with people returning from work. Their faces looked soft and warm in the golden light. Berka loved them all. Even that thief Steinberg who gave short weight in his butchery; and Chidrawi, the swarthy Syrian who was arranging a pyramid of yellow peaches in his window; and Levin the outfitter who stood in his doorway, a tape measure around his neck. And all those children outside the fish and chips shop watching wistfully as Ronnie Davis sprinkled vinegar over someone else's chips. He even felt a fleeting affection for the miser Pinn who owned the second-hand shop. His wife stood in the doorway, fluffing her hair this way and that, before embarking on what must be a two-hour journey home. She stopped off all along Main Street, garnering the news of the day, which she then embellished and disseminated among the housewives of First Avenue. She often knew better than they what was happening in the house next door. Some people were entirely unlovable.

Berka looked into the dark interior of Nathan's Drapery Store where his daughter Raizel worked. She was probably cashing up now. She had worked for the Nathans for four years, since she matriculated. At first she was a counter hand, measuring out elastic, hair ribbons and dress material. Today she practically ran the business. Mrs. Nathan spent most of her time in the city, drinking tea at the Corner Lounge, or walking about from shop to shop. Getting ideas for the trade, she called it. Mr. Nathan was almost blind. My eyes, he called Raizel. My heart, Berka murmured as he passed the shop.

The barbershop next to Nathan's was crowded with miners. Not, God forbid, having haircuts, but placing bets for the dog races.

Friday Night is Wanderers Night,
Night for Greyhound Racing.

read a poster on the wall. Next to it hung a framed picture

16

of water-waved ladies. And Wednesday night was Wembley Night, yet another night for dog racing.

Berka walked resolutely past the hotel bar. The Siren-sounds of clinking glasses and loud laughter would not tempt him tonight.

From the bar onwards Main Street ran a flat course for half a mile towards the large bluegum plantation which flanked the suburb on the west. The plantation stretched from the end of Main Street southwards towards the mine dumps. Below the dumps was a small dam into which water was pumped from underground. If Berka had seen snow-capped mountains, pine forests and an inland lake as he turned the corner from Main Street into First Avenue, he would not have been happier. He remembered when the first saplings had been planted. He had watched the mine dump grow as the coco-pans crawled up its sandy slopes depositing yet another load of finely crushed rock onto the chalky hill. And next to it the yellow slimes dam also grew slowly, hardening towards its final shape as a truncated pyramid.

He never tired of this constant yet ever-changing scene. On rainy days the dump stained deep yellow, the trees washed a lighter green and the leaden skies reflected dully in the cyanic dam. Under the clear winter skies the dam sparkled like a jewel, and the whiteness of the dump was blinding. He loved it most at sunset, however, when the dump became a mountain of gold dust and the dam liquid amber.

They could keep their gold bars in their vaults. He was satisfied with the refuse. From the top of First Avenue he surveyed his kingdom. King of the Rubbish Heaps, he thought with a smile. Beyond the veld which separated Mayfontein from the mine, the wheels of the headgear turned ceaselessly and the stentorian voice of the crushers echoed throughout the suburb, day and night, week after week, year after year, until it seemed to be the very breath of the suburb. He breathed in unison with it.

At this time of the day the rows of the red-bricked semi-detached houses glowed like live coals and the whole suburb caught fire. Only the plane trees cast a cooling shadow across the hot sandy roads. Yanka the fruit vendor came into view, driving his horses hard in his effort to reach home before the sabbath. Billowing clouds of red dust rose in his wake. Like the cumulus clouds which hung over the dump, like the dust raised by Boers on commando.

'This is my world,' Berka sighed as he walked down First Avenue towards his house, 'and I'm glad of it.'

2

'*I* should've had that drink!' Berka looked regretfully up First Avenue then back again to the veranda where Yenta, her ample bosom resting on its polished ledge, was waiting for him. Her hair was combed and she was wearing her best brown dress. That could mean one of two things: that she wanted a favour from him in which case she would have overlooked his beery breath, or that she had unpleasant news, in which case he would need a drink.

'Benjamin's in for the week-end,' she greeted him apologetically. 'He's come to see a doctor. Please be patient with him, Berrala. He's a sick man.'

Berrala. A man had as many names as his wife had moods. He was Berka when she talked about him to others; Berra when she was annoyed with him which was most of the time; Bernard when he had been to the bar with his non-Jewish friends, and Berrala when she wanted something from him. In her fantasies she undoubtedly saw him sitting in a plush office with 'Bernard K. Feldman' gilded on his door. If he did not have a middle name, she'd provide one.

'That's not all.' She put a restraining hand on his sleeve as he brushed past impatiently. 'Ruthie's in the lounge with that scabby dog of hers, Zutzke.'

Berka stopped. His gruffness could not hide his concern.

'What now?' he asked.

'This afternoon,' Yenta said replacing her bosom on the ledge, assured of his attention, 'when Gittel went out to feed the chickens, she noticed a piece of roof missing from the chicken run. And the chicken she'd been fattening for Purim had flown.'

'So?'

'So poor Gittel chased all over First Avenue looking for the silly chicken. She finally found it on Reb Hershl's kitchen table, pecking at the farfel which Faigel had put out to dry.'

'So now we've completed the saga of the chicken. What about Ruth?'

'Wait. Sheinka at the same time noticed that Ruth and Zutzke were missing. She went to the veld where Ruth had run away last time and saw her, followed by the dog, climbing up the mine dump. She was dragging that piece of corrugated iron behind her, like a sled. When she saw Sheinka, she fled into the plantation as though a horde of Cossacks were after her. Pregnant as she is, Sheinka dragged herself across the wet veld and found Ruth lying under the trees, crying her heart out. She wouldn't say why. You know a mother's heart: Sheinka feared she'd been raped by those wild mine kaffirs . . .'

'Stop talking like a stupid yiddine. So what happened then?'

'So what happened then he asks. Nothing.' Yenta hated interruptions. She liked to tell a story in her own time, with suitable digressions. But she remembered that Benjamin was in from the Free State and controlled her temper. 'So what happened? Ruth ranted like a meshugene about pogroms, blood and snow. The piece of iron, she said, was her sled and she was running away from the Cossacks. Then she ran away from Sheinka. She's been in the lounge for the last hour, waiting for you.'

Yenta looked grave. Berka hated the gravity, the muted tones in which they spoke about Ruth. As though the child were an idiot, a cripple.

He walked into the dark airless passage from which all the rooms in the house led off. It had pockets of smells which evoked the week's meals: pickled brisket, sauerkraut, cauliflower, gefilte fish, not to mention the all-pervading smell of pickling cucumbers and fermenting wine. He screwed up his nose and lit his pipe. In the far corner of the lounge Ruth lay sprawled out in a large armchair, her ginger head against Zutke's spotted one. They were both asleep.

Berka sat down on a chair near the door. He really needed a drink but he'd wait for Raizel. When she came home she would pour him a schnapps and amuse him with tales about Nathan's. A perceptive girl, his Raizel. Perhaps he should have let her become a teacher. In the five years that Dovid had gone to night school he had not learned as much English as in the last year when Raizel had begun to teach him. But Berka had been afraid; so many teachers remain old maids.

With boys it was different. They needed a trade, a profession. Yenta had wanted their son Joel to be a doctor. When he had apprenticed himself to a pharmacist, Yenta consoled herself: They understand more than doctors, these chemists, she said. When I've got a pain, a cold, anything, I go to Brown the chemist, he gives me a mixture and in a few days I'm as strong as a horse again. What's so marvellous about doctors? In the old country the sick died of their diseases and the doctor died of starvation. Please God when Joel finishes, I'll give him with what to start his own little chemist shop.

Towards this end Yenta had been pickling cucumbers and fermenting wine in the cellar for years. Her products were snapped up by the neighbours and by Sharp's Delicatessen as soon as they matured. How's Joel's little chemist shop coming along, Berka would ask with heavy sarcasm. His earnings had kept them in relative comfort during all the years of their married life but he did not have a penny in the bank. Laugh, laugh, Yenta would reply. One day you'll see.

Joel's boss was complimentary about him. So charming with the clients, he told Berka. Clients yet; he, Berka, had customers. And so charming. For that he got an education? He wished Joel would shed a little more charm at home. Since he was asked out to his rich clients' homes he had grown so high and mighty. Bring your friends here one Friday night, Yenta had offered in her innocence. You must reciprocate. I'll make noodle soup, tzimmes, a stuffed duck.

Berka had watched Joel take in her untidy hair, her ill-fitting false teeth which clattered loosely as she spoke, her nails which were blackened from the coal stove and from her wine making. He followed Joel's eyes down to Berka's slippers which she always wore. I can't ma, he told her turning away. We're not geared for visitors. Bring them, bring them, I can manage. Last Pesach I had twenty people here for the seder. I can . . . She had broken off abruptly, rubbed her nose

21

vigorously and ended lamely: Oh, I understand. Well, perhaps we do need new curtains. And the sofa is a little worn . . .

That was education for you.

Their house did look shabby. The lace curtains were yellow with dust, the floral linoleum needed a good scrubbing and the heavy rust-coloured settee and armchairs threw up clouds of dust when one sat down. Phthisis one could get. But Yenta would not spring-clean until Passover. This vestigial behaviour stemmed from the old country where the housewives waited for the long cold winter to pass and for the snows to melt before they took down their curtains, polished the windows and scrubbed the floors. The fact that Passover occurred in autumn in South Africa, not in the spring, did not deflect Yenta from her girlhood rituals.

It was hard to keep the mine dust out of the house. In the dry winter months the wind whipped up the loose sand from the dumps, covering everything and everyone with a fine layer of dust. Yet Sheinka and Gittel, Yenta's sister, managed to keep their house clean. Like a chemist shop — Yenta herself said. But it was to Yenta's house that the visitors flocked, not to Gittel's. They dropped in for a chat, for a game of klabberjas; they sat on the veranda in summer and around the kitchen stove in winter. There was always enough to eat for those who were tardy in leaving at mealtimes. Everyone responded to Yenta's warmth and kindness, and ignored the smells, the dust and the general untidiness of the house. They visited Gittel and Sheinka only by invitation.

But she could keep the place cleaner, Berka brooded. The only pretty thing in the lounge was a vase of marigolds which Raizel had put on the little glass table. When he suggested to Yenta that she take in a native servant she said: I don't want blacks in the house; they stink.

Her cucumbers and her wine didn't stink. Berka struck a match. Ruth stirred. She's emotionally exhausted, Berka thought as she moaned quietly and fell asleep again. Since her tonsilectomy she suffered badly from nightmares. They're choking me, they're choking me! she'd cry leaping out of bed. They said they'd take out my tonsils with a teaspoon, she told Berka reproachfully when she came out of hospital. A big light shone on me. They put a black smelly thing over my nose and I couldn't breathe. Afterwards I knew I wasn't dead because my throat was so sore. They didn't take them out with a spoon. And they didn't give me ice cream and jelly afterwards like mamma said.

Like an orphan they treated her. To have left a sensitive seven-year-old all alone in the hospital; Berka still couldn't get over it. Yenta had taken Ruth into hospital by tram and Raizel had brought her home next day in a taxi. Dovid was working, Sheinka was pregnant and Gittel couldn't speak English.

Berka's pipe went out again. He did not risk lighting another match. He put the pipe into the ashtray and looked at the pictures on the wall. Yenta's sepia-tinted mother and father hung above the settee in matching oval frames. Their features had been blurred by time and enlargement and they could have been anybody's mother and father. The mother, a dark round-faced woman, wore a wig. The father's face was covered with a long beard, a thick moustache and a forelock which was combed low over his forehead. Only his large brown eyes — like Raizel's — were visible above an aquiline nose. He wore a yarmulka.

The other walls were covered with haughty uncles and smug aunts under whose noses Berka longed to draw big black moustaches. Yenta was proud of her family. They certainly had had the time and money to make frequent visits to the photographer.

Berka marvelled at the speed with which his feelings of universal love and tolerance dissipated when he stepped into his house. He smiled, however, when he looked at the picture of Raizel and Joel as children. Even Joel looked lovable.

There were photographs of picnics in Lithuanian woods, of the village choir, of the river. There was also a street scene in Ragaza, a broad sandy road with little wooden houses under shingled roofs; a horse and cart in the distance and an occasional tree growing in a garden. Berka had often seen Ruth standing in front of this picture, staring at it, almost fearfully.

On the wall behind him was a wedding photo of Dovid and Sheinka. She looked dark and lovely and he proud and studious. A pair of gold-rimmed glasses rested lightly on his nose. Berka smiled. Dovid's eyesight was as good as his own.

The gold-rimmed glasses and the book under the arm were the emblems of the Lithuanian intellectual. They carried the best literature under their arms.

There were no pictures of Berka's family. These had been destroyed together with everything else. To look at the walls one would think he had been born from a stone.

To his right were his and Yenta's wedding pictures. They were separate and had not been taken at their wedding but Berka insisted on calling them his wedding pictures. One was a picture of Yenta and her sister Gittel. Gittel's round pretty face was in the full light. Her hair was draped back into a soft chignon and she smiled with the assurance of a pretty woman. Yenta's face receded into the dark background. Her beaked nose was skilfully touched up by the photographer and her intelligent scornful smile acknowledged that she was a foil for her older sister's good looks. Only her large brown eyes — again like Raizel's — brightened up her long dark face.

This was the picture with which Benjamin had wooed Berka on her behalf. The other one is prettier, he agreed, but she's eight years older and she's married. Yenta may not be the most beautiful woman in the world but what a character she's got, what a character! And what a character she turned out to have. Berka should have been warned by that all-knowing smile.

Next to it hung the second half of the wedding picture, the one of Berka which Benjamin had sent to Yenta. He stood in front of a mining magnate's house and his features were sacrificed to background. He leaned possessively against an ornate iron gate, his thumb lightly hooked into the chain of a watch — kindly lent by the photographer. His hair was parted in the centre and his moustache, which he later trimmed down to Yenta's specifications, stretched from ear to ear, like his smile.

'I thought the house belonged to you,' Yenta would throw up at him in later matrimonial disputes.

'And I thought you had character,' he countered. 'Looks I could see you didn't have.'

'So, who asked you to bring me out from Ragaza?'

'Your brother. And I was tired of wandering about. They all said I needed a good Jewish wife, a home. Some home you made me. A bed of nails.'

'If not for me you wouldn't have had nails either.'

'I should have married Maria du Toit. Her father promised me the farm when he died.'

'You deserve a goya. You're a peasant. Who else but a poor orphan like me, living with her married sister, would have come out to a strange country to marry an even stranger man?'

'On your holy brother's recommendation. For once he showed good judgement, on your behalf. And tell me: Who brought out your sister and her children to South Africa when her husband died? Benjamin or me?'

'Who said you didn't? Will you throw that up at me for the rest of my life?'

Berka sighed. He never won an argument with Yenta. She was convinced that he disliked Benjamin because he had been instrumental in their marriage. She could not conceive of the fact that Benjamin was a repulsive human being in his own right.

Berka heard a light shuffle of feet behind him. Yenta stood in the passage with a large cup of coffee in her hand, motioning him towards the veranda. Benjamin was probably staying all week. He got up quietly and followed her. She waited until he had settled himself in the cane chair before she handed him the strong sweet coffee. Then she leaned against the veranda ledge again, looking expectantly up the street.

Raizel was due home, her sabbath dinner was ready and when Benjamin returned from synagogue they would eat. Not that the sabbath dinner differed much from weekday meals. Berka had discouraged her years ago from making a fuss of the sabbath. A white table cloth and her mother's silver candlesticks were the only concessions to tradition which Berka, after many battles, had allowed her.

The sun had already set behind the plantation and the air was fresh and cool. The smell of warm damp earth and bruised marigolds mingled with that of sabbath cooking which floated down the street. On every block from the top of Main Street to the end of First Avenue, lived at least two Jewish families. On their own block there was their landlady Mrs. Zaidman and her spinster daughter; the Schwartzmans and Dovid's family. Over the road lived the Pinns and Reb Hershl's family. They were surrounded by friends. Except, of course, for their new neighbours, the Burgers.

Berka sipped his coffee loudly then listened. Old man Burger sat just behind the wall which separated their verandas. He was also drinking coffee, noisily. He had moved into the other half of the semi-detached house a few months ago. A balding bull-necked man with a red angry face, he had barely returned Berka's greetings since he moved in. His wife and six children — goodness only knew where they all slept in their two-bedroomed house — were no friendlier. Only their eldest son Jan whom he often met in the bar, greeted him politely.

Perhaps Hershl was right. He would have to revise his ideas of Boer friendliness and hospitality.

The Burgers were urbanised Afrikaners but the dedication with which the old man tended his garden made Berka suspect that he had once been a farmer. All the other houses had crushed stone from the mines covering their tiny patch of garden. Burger dug and manured the soil, planted sweet-smelling flowers, bushes and creepers, and spent all his free time either in the garden or hammering in the cellar which he had converted into a workshop.

Aaron Blecher and his family had been very different neighbours. Trust his wife to drag him off to a 'better' suburb, to provide a good address for their marriageable daughters. When they left, Berka lost an invaluable klabberjas hand and Yenta a close friend. The low backyard wall which divided their houses had hummed with a constant traffic of loaned cups of oil, flour and sugar. Now Yenta was greeted by the implacable pale face of Mrs. Burger. In spite of this Yenta still wanted to buy the house they had lived in for the past twenty years.

'Mrs. Zaidman was here again today,' she said as she took away Berka's empty cup. 'She only wants a hundred pounds down, the rest to be paid in monthly instalments. She says . . .'

'She's selling cheap because she needs hard cash for her krasavitza's dowry,' Berka said irritably.

'Molly's not ugly and she's not unmarriageable. She's only twenty-seven.'

'Not counting Mondays and Thursdays.'

'She wouldn't even sell it, but since her husband died . . .'

'Forget it, Yenta. I'm not going into real estate.'

Yenta sighed. Why did she persist? She and Berka had discovered long ago just how far they could push one another. In fact, they understood one another so well that there seemed little point in talking at all. The turbulent days of their marriage when Mrs. Pinn on her veranda could report word for word of an argument taking place in their own kitchen, were over. If they argued now it was simply a matter of form, to acknowledge that the other existed.

'I had the strangest dream last night,' Yenta changed the subject. She rarely had ordinary dreams. 'I dreamed I ordered two baskets of black grapes from Yanka to make wine. His horse ate half of one basket. I was so angry that I went to the Syrian and he delivered two baskets to the house. As I sat down to press them into the wine barrel, I discovered that there were cucumbers in the baskets, not grapes.'

'And so?' Berka asked, waiting for the inevitable interpretation of signs and portents which always had a bearing on dog racing.

'The double for tonight will be two and two,' she said. 'I've already placed a bet.'

'Foolish woman. One of the baskets was half empty. The double for tonight will be two and one and a half. Or, if you add the Syrian's baskets to Yanka's and subtract . . .'

'Another Joseph!' she said with infinite contempt. 'Go tell it to Pharaoh.'

She watched Mrs. Pinn's progress down the street. Yenta had seen her turning into First Avenue when she went into the kitchen to make coffee for Berka. So far she had only covered three quarters of the street, describing a zig-zag course as she crossed from one house to another. To beat a hasty retreat into the house as Mrs. Pinn approached meant you had something to hide. To receive her with equanimity was a sure sign of a clear conscience. Unlike the Angel of Death she passed over all the non-Jewish houses, stopping only at her co-religionists'. The goyim's gossip, it seemed, was not worth collecting.

Tonight her stops were shorter than usual. Mrs. Pinn observed the sabbath and she wanted to be home in time to light the candles.

'Have you seen mine Raizel?' Yenta asked when she finally arrived at her veranda. She always spoke English to Mrs. Pinn although the latter, who was born in South Africa, had learned to speak Yiddish after the first lot of immigrants arrived from Lithuania. In a suburb of immigrants Yiddish was an occupational imperative.

'Oh yes,' Mrs. Pinn answered in her gritty voice. She felt slighted by Berka's curt nod. 'She was walking slowly along Main Street with Mr. Erlich. They seemed in no great hurry to get home.'

She watched Berka for a reaction. When she got none, she gave Yenta her news: They said the Syrian had rejected Yanka's offer for his fruit shop. He wanted an extra hundred pounds' goodwill. They said that Reb Hershl had made a secret offer for Sharp's Delicatessen. As an old friend she was tipping off Yenta to approach Reb Hershl about selling him her cucumbers. The rebbetzim, they said, had already offered him wine for the Passover. They also said that Schumacher, the German refugee who had opened an ice-cream shop next to the police station, was only half-Jewish and that his wife was a full-blooded German, a terrible anti-semite. She for one would not buy his ice-cream. Who knew what they put into it?

'They say,' Berka mumbled angrily, walking into the house. 'They say. Who the hell is They?'

'They say,' Mrs. Pinn continued, disconcerted by Berka's abrupt withdrawal but refusing to be silenced, 'that Yaakov Koren has stopped sending money to his wife and child and that they're living on charity from the shtetl. He's sending her a divorce instead and he's going to marry the widow Kagan before Rosh Hashana.'

When Berka came into the lounge he found Ruth sitting upright in the chair, a dazed sleepy expression on her face. Zutzke was stretching himself luxuriously at her feet. She smiled happily as Berka picked her up and she put her thin arms around his neck. The smell of bluegums and acidic dump sand clung to her curly ginger hair. He hugged her warmly then sat on the armchair, holding her in his lap.

'Ruthie's had a hard day. Tell me about it,' he said softly in Yiddish.

She leaned contentedly against his chest, saying nothing.

'Tell Zeide Berka what you did today, Ruthie.'

'I, I don't know if I dreamed it or if it really happened,' she said with a frown.

'Tell me the dream then. Bobbe Yenta always tells me her dreams. Maybe if I know what you dreamed we'll be able to work out the double for tonight's dog racing.'

Ruth smiled. Everybody knew about Yenta's dreams.

'It was like last time,' she began, hiding her head on Berka's shoulder. 'I dreamed, I think I dreamed, that I heard horses and I knew that I must run away. In the snow it's hard without a sled, so I took the iron from Bobbe Gittel's chicken run. And I ran to the, dumps, to the snow mountain. With the lake and the forest, like Daddy told me.'

She dug her face into his shoulder again and was quiet for a while.

'And it happened again, like last time. It didn't look like Mayfontein. It looked like that picture on the wall, that one,' she pointed without looking at the street scene of Ragaza. 'All the houses were on fire and those men with the big swords came on horses and, and . . .' She burst into tears.

'Finish, my child. Then it will be over and out.'

'And they killed everybody who was running out of the houses. And the snow in the street was red,' she blurted out, 'and I ran into the forest.'

Berka sat, silent with guilt, holding her tightly against his chest.

'And I didn't know if I dreamed it or thought it or if it really happened,' Ruth said. 'And Mamma shouted and hit me and said I was a liar.'

'Shah, shah. It did happen, my poor child, but not to you. To someone else and a very long time ago. It is all over now and it will never happen again, so you mustn't worry. It will never never happen again.'

He sat very still until he felt all the tension leave her thin body. Then he heard a loud voice on the veranda. Within seconds Sheinka had rushed into the lounge, preceded by a strong smell of Vicks.

'I knew she'd be here, the little liar! Steals the iron off the roof to play dangerous games on the dumps, then tells silly stories about pogroms. She's either crazy and doesn't know what she's talking about or she's an out and out liar. Come home immediately!'

Ruth clung to Berka.

'Quietly, quietly,' Berka told Sheinka sternly. 'I've just managed to calm her.'

'It's you and Dovid who fill her head with nonsense!' Sheinka cried. 'Stories, stories, stories! No wonder the child's an idiot. She doesn't know what or where she is half the time.'

'Sit down, Sheinkala, and don't excite yourself. Remember your health,' Berka said quietly.

At the mention of her health Sheinka collapsed into a chair with one hand over her heart and the other over her stomach.

'The baby will be born dead, I know it!' she wailed. 'How can any living thing survive such upsets? And it will be her fault.'

Ruth tensed up against Berka and looked at him in mute appeal. He tightened his hold on her.

'Yenta, bring Sheinkala a cup of that delicious hot coffee,' he said.

'No. I'm going home. Come,' she said to Ruth as she wriggled out of the chair.

Ruth turned around slowly to face her mother and said haltingly, in English.

'I don't want to go home mit you.'

Sheinka fell back into the chair. Her face crumbled as she cried: 'In English! Did you hear? She spoke to me in English! What am I, a stranger? Gott in Himmel! What sin have I committed to deserve such a strange child?'

3

*D*ovid looked towards the mine dumps over which the sun was setting. It was all so ugly: The sun like an evil eye in the red sky; the yellow sand; the turgid water. Even the birds recoiled from that foul-smelling pool and the silent bluegum plantation at its edge. The trees were dull green all year round and smelled of eucalyptus. Like Sheinka. They did not shed their leaves in winter nor put out new ones in spring. Like everything else in Africa they looked artificial. Here the earth seemed governed by laws which did not respond to a benign nature. Forests were planted, mountains built from mine refuse and lakes pumped up from hell. Dovid shuddered. And that infernal headgear just kept turning and turning. One's very soul felt lashed to its wheels.

Out of the corner of his eye he saw Berka walking into the bakery with his arm around Hershl's shoulders. Berka loved the country. Johannesburg's not Africa, he frequently told Dovid, describing the rolling grasslands, the mountains, the valleys. But Johannesburg does have a beauty of its own, he said. Perhaps. Dovid could not see it. If his father, Red Yehuda, had remained in Africa twenty-five years ago instead of returning to the old country, Dovid might have grown up with a different view of Africa.

Yehuda, like other Jews from Lithuania, had come to the diamond diggings in 1912 to seek his fortune. He went for one year but stayed two. "Noch a yahr in Africa," he wrote to his wife, prolonging his stay. Another year in Africa, in exile. He returned to Ragaza with two hundred pounds and a

31

golden brooch for his wife. South Africa, he told her when she suggested emigrating, had no future. After the gold had been extracted from the earth all the adventurers would leave and the veld would come into its own again. How could he take his family to a land where the earth was sour from the gold in its veins, where the hills were rocky and bare and where the rivers ran shallow and brown? Nowhere had he seen green fields and forests like those of Ragaza nor a river which flowed through such fragrant banks.

Eighteen years later Dovid, under pressure from Sheinka, was the only member of his family to emigrate. Yehuda had not lived to see him go. Dovid found Johannesburg as bleak and as bare as his father had described it. But Yehuda had been wrong about one thing: South Africa, it seemed, did have a future. Whether or not Dovid wanted to be a part of it was another matter.

Dovid pressed his head against the cool glass. His family in Lithuania did not understand what life was like in Africa. They believed that the streets were paved with the proverbial gold. I hear, his mother wrote bitterly, that in addition to your wife and child you also support Gittel. For your own mother, however, you haven't got a few roubles to send. You've forgotten how I slaved into the small hours of the night to support you and your brothers while your father was seeking fortunes in Africa . . .

Would they believe him if he wrote that last month he had to borrow three pounds towards the rent from Steinberg the butcher? He sent money home when he could. As explanations proved futile his letters to his mother became less frequent. But one day he'd go home again and the need for explanations would cease.

He glanced away from the mine dumps. Berka and Hershl were standing outside the bakery looking up at him. He pretended not to see them. Only when Berka turned homewards did he look down the road in the direction of Nathan's Drapery Store. It was ten past five. Raizel was probably cashing up. He had time to sew the buttons onto the jacket.

Crazy, he was absolutely crazy. Here he was, thirty-one, with a school-going daughter, an ailing pregnant wife and her parasitic family to support and what was he doing? Daydreaming like a lovesick adolescent.

He walked angrily across the wooden boards and pulled off an unfinished suit from the hanger. The left lapel needed adjustment. His perfectionism maddened Sheinka. You could turn out two extra suits a month if you weren't so meticulous, she complained. Look at Yaakov Koren. A rich man he's becoming from his tailoring.

He looked at Yaakov Koren; a mere haizenschneider, a trouser maker, who couldn't even sew a sleeve into a jacket.

His hands shook as he wound the cotton onto the bobbin. He threaded the needle with difficulty and placed the lapel under the presser foot. For a while he sat staring at his old Singer machine, with his foot poised over the treadle, then he got up and went to the window again.

'Raizel, I love you,' he whispered fiercely against the window, misting it with his breath. So. He had said it at last and the skies had not fallen onto his head.

She had been a child of fifteen when he arrived in Johannesburg, a lively precocious girl who had giggled at his English. He dismissed her as an unpleasant child but was stung by her laughter. He watched her grow out of her adolescent gawkishness into a rounded young woman whom all the neighbourhood boys pursued. He often walked into Berka's house to hear the gramophone blaring out a tango and was pained to watch some young lout bending over her as he led her through the intricate steps. His pain was for Berka, he had told himself. One day he would have trouble with that girl. She's only a child, he reproached himself afterwards. And he clung to this comforting phrase which allowed him to ignore her blossoming womanhood.

One cold winter's evening about eighteen months ago, Dovid had been sitting in front of the coal stove with Ruth on his lap. He was alone. Gittel and Sheinka had gone to visit Yenta. In the glow of the sabbath candles Dovid sang Yiddish songs for Ruth. He sang of workers who built mansions for the rich but themselves lived in hovels; who sewed for the idle and wore rags; who ploughed the fields but owned no land. There were songs about families parted by war, by poverty, by persecution; about refugees herded in cattle trucks, going into exile through snowy wastes. He sang of lonely orphans in a hostile world, and about crossed lovers. There seemed to be no other lovers in Yiddish folklore.

'Sing "Oyfn Pripetshok",' Ruth requested. Dovid sang about the Rabbi who teaches his pupils, with the first letters of the alphabet, that the world is a vale of tears:

> . . . As you grow older, dear children,
> All too soon you'll learn,
> How many tears the eye holds
> And how to weep and yearn . . .

'And now about the man who doesn't know when it's his birthday,' she said sleepily.

He sang about the man who had nothing by which to measure his years. The rich man measures his days by his money, the happy man by the passing hours. If misery were the measure of life, he would be ancient; if happiness were, he is not yet born.

> Eib leben heist laiden, dan leb ich shein lang,
> Dan hob ich genug shein die yahren,
> Eib leben heist heren fun glick chotz ein klang,
> Dan bin ich noch garnisht geboren.

Ruth knew all his songs. They took the place of bedtime stories. At least part of his heritage would live on, he thought gratefully as she slept in his arms.

What was he doing in this harsh alien land where he would always be a stranger? His life was bound up with der heim, the old country, where he was born, where his family lived, where his father lay buried. His fate was linked with theirs. Like his father before him he longed for the pinewoods of Ragaza, and for the river which flowed through such fragrant banks.

As he wiped away his tears, he heard a light step across the floor. He turned around, startled. Raizel stood behind him in the flickering candlelight with tears in her eyes. She bent down quickly, kissed him full on the lips, then fled.

Had it really happened, he wondered afterwards, or had it been a wraith from one of his songs? From Raizel he had no sign. She remained as lively and as provocative as ever. When she was not looking he searched her face, he hardly knew for what. For traces of tears he had seen in the candlelight? But he sensed she had changed, that she was conscious of him. Once, when Ruth asked whether only Jews lived in Russia, Raizel laughed and said that as a child she too had thought that Russia was a Jewish country; it was der heim for everyone she had known. Then she herself began to ask Dovid questions: about der heim, about Jewish festivals, about Jewish history. And the previous year she had offered to give him English lessons, to correct his pronunciation.

As the religious man works and battles through the week towards his soul's repose on the sabbath, so Dovid yearned for Sunday nights when he would sit at Berka's kitchen table, his books in front of him, listening to Raizel. Like this, she would say putting her tongue against her even white teeth. He turned from her with a hammering heart. You put your tongue so, then blow out: 'th', not 'd', this thing, not dis ding. Hey, you're not watching. You'll never learn if you keep your nose in the book. Look at me!

And when he turned to look, not at her mouth shaping a 'th' but into her eyes, he found what he was looking for.

Dovid moved away from the window and began to clear the room feverishly. He must hurry, he must hurry. He tore the jacket from under the presser foot, threw it over a hanger, then grabbing his own jacket, rushed out of his workshop down the flight of dark stone stairs, into the street.

The office in Nathan's Drapery Store stood on a glass-enclosed platform at the far end of the shop. Here Mrs. Nathan, in her working days, had sat at a desk beside Mr. Nathan, looking down sternly upon her domain. Raizel now sat at her desk. She opened the oblong capsule which had been sent on the pneumatic cable from Mrs. Cole at Napery, checked the invoice and gave the change. Mr. Nathan, in the meantime, walked slowly around the shop, his hands clasped behind his back.

Raizel longed to go home and soak the tiredness out of her limbs. It had been an exhausting week. She glanced at her watch. Quarter past five. If she hurried . . . No. She would not hurry. She would cash up, wait for Mrs. Cole and Gloria Brits to tidy up their counters, then remain on to discuss the week's takings with Mr. Nathan. He would be delighted. She must also tell him that she would be late on Monday morning because she was taking Ruthie to school.

Resentment welled up in her. Raizel will do it, her mother always offered. And that miserable Sheinka lay around all day with Vicks-soaked cotton wool on her chest and an injured look on her face.

I hate her, I hate her! I wish she were dead! Raizel raged inwardly, breaking a nail on the cash register.

It wasn't the child's fault. Poor Ruthie. Ruthie at school. She could hardly imagine it. No one realised how difficult it would be, how cruel children were. She had seen them form a ring around an unfortunate newcomer who still wore his trousers tucked into thick grey socks, Russian style. Bolshie! Bolshie! Isaac is a Bolshevik! they sang as they danced around the unfortunate boy who was trying to control his tears. Perhaps they would be gentler with a girl.

Father and child. How uncanny the resemblance was between them; the high pale forehead, dark brows beneath red hair, large green eyes, vulnerable, puzzled, the eyes of a perplexed child.

When she had come into the kitchen that night they looked so close that they might have been carved from one stone. In the glow of the candles they reminded her of a religious picture she had once seen.

For a long time she stood quietly in the dark, listening to Dovid's songs. She had always been irritated and bored by tales about der heim, the old country. The life there seemed so remote, so melancholy. But when Dovid sang songs or told tales, he opened up for her a world that was complete and beautiful. Purim, Chanukah, Pesach had had no meaning for her other than as festivals when one went to synagogue, heard the rabbi pray in an unintelligible tongue, then returned home to delicacies traditionally associated with these festivals: hammentashen, latkes, kneidlach.

When Dovid sang about these festivals, she caught a fleeting image of a past in which there was dignity, a passion for freedom and pride in ancient heroes. The songs of the shtetl were different, more accepting of sorrows and hardship. But they too had bound people together in adversity.

This was her past as well, and she wanted desperately to be part of it. She existed only in the present, a heritage which her father had foisted upon her. He needed to cut himself off from his painful past; she needed to acquire one. She envied those who belonged and believed: the girls at the convent with the crosses around their necks, the Jewish girls walking to synagogue together. Her father had made religion unattractive for her at an early age. The hypocrites! he raged about seasonal shul-goers. They don't even understand what they're praying about. Or to whom. A merciful, all-knowing, all-loving God indeed! A vindictive, punishing God, that's who!

He had taken away the possibility of God and given her nothing in its place.

He scoffed at Dovid's love for the Jewish past. A singer, a dreamer, he said, full of inconsistent ideas. But Raizel understood that things were not clear-cut for Dovid because he allowed himself to doubt. He loved Jewish tradition but could not believe in God. He was intensely involved in Jewish life but longed for what he called the brotherhood of all men. His nostalgia for der heim had another dimension: He felt that he was missing out on the greatest experiment in human history, a real socialist revolution.

He stood somewhere between Hershl and Berka in the unending arguments which began on the veranda in summer and continued around the kitchen table in winter. Hershl nodded his approval when Dovid spoke about the wonder of Jewish survival throughout the centuries, attributing it to their passionate adherence to the Torah.

'Fool!' Berka would shout him down. 'They'd have survived better if they had merged with the people around them, instead of shutting themselves off with their holy books in the ghettoes.'

'The German Jews are still trying that,' Hershel interpolated quietly. 'But the Nazis are keeping them Jewish.'

'You're speaking about a political aberration, not a law of history,' Berka answered heatedly.

But Dovid disagreed with Hershl that there was a contradiction in being a traditional Diaspora Jew and a devout socialist. He laughed at his suggestion that such a combination would only succeed in a Jewish State. Dovid was not a Zionist.

Raizel did not understand many of their arguments. She only knew that when Dovid spoke it seemed right. And when he sang the sad songs about der heim and the rousing ones about Jewish heroes and workers, the melodies reconciled any contradiction which the words might contain.

She had watched Dovid wipe away his tears that evening and wanted desperately to become a part of his world, the key to which he carried within himself. Hardly aware of what she was doing, she ran across the kitchen floor, put her arms around his neck and kissed him full on the lips.

'Mr. Nathan!' she called across the shop. 'Is it all right if I leave now? I'll be in early tomorrow morning.'

As she stepped out of the shop she saw Dovid rush out of his building, his tie awry, his hair, redder in the dying light of the sun, falling over his forehead. He stopped when he saw her, put on his jacket and crossed the street slowly. She, in the meantime, had turned towards Chidrawi's fruit shop. They met at the door.

'Is your building on fire?' she asked.

'Yes. No!' He looked away. 'I mean, you know how it is on Fridays. The week's at an end and one gets tired of working.'

'Don't they look marvellous!' She pointed to the pyramid of yellow cling peaches which Chidrawi had arranged in his window.

'I don't like strange fruit. Peaches have hairy skins and they set my teeth on edge. Nor do I like bananas or pawpaws, and grapes remind me of my childhood illnesses. They were supposed to have curative properties in the old country. Give me pears and apples any time. And those wild strawberries! What a scent they had.'

'I want to buy some peaches, wait for me,' Raizel said, happy to find him in an outgoing mood. There were times when they walked home together without exchanging more than a dozen words.

Mrs. Pinn was in the shop, leaning on Chidrawi's counter, a small brown paper bag in her hand. You should see her choose fruit, Chidrawi often complained to Raizel. Everything she touches and squeezes. And she chooses her cabbages from the bottom of the pile. When she leaves after spending a few pence, I have to begin building it up again. But I don't complain. If I did, there'd be a rumour in Mayfontein that I cheat with the change or that I sell rotten fruit.

'Yanka is a stupid stingy man,' Childrawi was telling Mrs. Pinn, certain that the message would reach him. 'He'll ride around on his horse and cart like a coolie all his life if he doesn't cough up another hundred pounds. I worked for fifteen years to build up my business . . . Oh hello, Miss Feldman,' he said turning to Raizel with a smile.

'Goodbye Mr. Chidrawi,' Mrs. Pinn said after greeting Raizel coolly. 'And don't keep Miss Feldman long. She has a gentleman waiting for her outside.'

Raizel watched her walk up to Dovid who reddened at something she said. He looked after her in anger as she walked away. He was still upset when Raizel came out of the shop.

'What did she say?' Raizel asked.

'Nothing,' he answered abruptly, his happy mood destroyed.

Raizel took his arm but he sprang away as though he had been stung.

'Don't do that,' he muttered, looking around anxiously. 'There are people all around us.'

'May I do it when they're not?' she asked brightly, suppressing her tears. He had never reacted like this before.

'For you everything's a joke. Why don't you act like a grown woman?'

'Because you keep telling me I'm only a child.'

'Don't you understand?' he appealed. 'To fall into Mrs. Pinn's black pit of a mouth is just about the worst thing that can happen to a young girl.'

'Or to a married man. Look at Yaakov Koren. I'd tear her mouth to pieces if I fell into it and she knows it, the old sow. What did she say, Dovid? It's upset you. You've nothing to be ashamed of.'

'Nothing,' he echoed.

They walked on in silence until they reached the barbershop. Dovid slowed down, looking into the brightly-lit shop. It was full of miners in their working clothes who were pushing money towards Sam, the barber. He sat at a small table making notes in a little book. The barber's chair stood like an empty throne in the centre of the shop.

'Samke and the dog racing,' Dovid said, frowning. 'He should try working for a living.'

'At least his family eats. Look at those poor kids,' she said, pointing to two bare-footed boys with their younger sister who were sitting on the pavement outside the bar. Their clothes were grubby and their feet caked with mud. The boy in the centre held a packet of chips and solemnly doled out one at a time to his brother and sister. 'They're probably waiting for their father to come out of the bar.'

Just then the doors of the bar swung open and a tall blond man stepped out. He stared at Raizel insolently, made a mock bow and said:

'Good afternoon, Miss Feldman. Did you like my flowers?'

'Thank you,' she nodded. 'Don't denude your father's garden for me.'

'It's a pleasure.'

'Isn't that Burger's son, our new neighbour?' Dovid asked as they walked away. 'He looks like a Russian peasant.' He turned around. Jan Burger was still standing at the swinging door, staring after them. 'Such bold eyes he has. What flowers was he talking about?'

'He's been asking me to go out with him since they moved in. Now that's material for Mrs. Pinn. And yesterday he picked some marigolds from his father's garden for me. My father should only know where the flowers are from!'

'Charming,' Dovid said, controlling his voice. 'What does he do for a living?'

'I hardly know him. Mrs. Pinn says he's an electrician on the mine. I loved chips when I was a child,' she changed the subject abruptly. 'What was your favourite food?'

'Anything that filled the stomach. For long periods our staple diet was herring and potatoes. But on Friday nights it was different. My mother would be up at dawn to make delicious yeast buns with cinnamon. In better times we had cheese cakes too. But no matter how poor we were she always baked extra for the beggars who came around on Friday afternoons.'

When Raizel saw the dreamy look on his face she knew that he had forgotten Mrs. Pinn and Jan Burger. He leaned towards her, speaking eagerly.

'Did I ever tell you about Meishe, my oldest brother? He's a remarkable person, always active in communal affairs and politics. He overrode the objections of the bigots and got the Party to send out a teacher from Vilna. Vera Ostrovskaya started our first secular school in Schleima-Janka's barn. Her pupils were grown men whose education had stopped with their barmitzvahs. The religious people were horrified: To learn Russian or science or history; to neglect the Torah, was to be well on the road to apostasy.'

Raizel had heard about the teacher from Sheinka. A frowsy old maid Sheinka once told her, whose petticoat hung out and whose stockings twisted around her ankles. Dovid was besotted with her, Sheinka said. Before he knew me of course. When I decided I wanted Dovid, that old blue stocking didn't have a chance.

'Was she old, this teacher?' Raizel asked.

'Oh no. I was then about twenty and she must have been twenty-three or twenty-four. Most of her pupils were older than her. She was a very dedicated young woman. I, I'm afraid I didn't treat her too well,' he admitted, shamefaced. 'We were sort of engaged. Then Sheinka turned up and before I knew it, that was that.'

'Did girls also go to the school in the barn?' Raizel asked.

'A few did, but most of the others, like Sheinka, only joined the choir or came to the socials. They didn't think they could learn anything from a woman,' he smiled. 'I did. So did the others. She started a class in Russian literature. It was she who introduced me to Tolstoy, Dostoevsky and the other Russian writers. How are you finding "Anna Karenina" by the way?'

'Marvellous!' Raizel said. 'I know just how she feels. What an uncompromising love! What courage! And what terrible conflicts she must have had to leave her son.'

'There's more to the book than the love story,' Dovid said with some irritation. Give a woman a complete world view and she'll extract from it only what she needs. Vera Ostrovskaya was the only woman he had ever known who saw life in wider terms than love, marriage and procreation.

When Raizel saw him smile she knew that he had retreated into his private world from which she was excluded. She walked silently at his side and made no further effort at conversation.

They turned into First Avenue. The sun had disappeared behind the plantation, a cool breeze had come up, and a new moon was rising in an amethyst sky. They walked down the middle of the road, damp from the afternoon's rain, whose surface bore traces of recent hoof and wheel marks.

'Everyone's on their verandas, enjoying the cool evening,' Raizel said.

Dovid drew away from Raizel again. He felt he was on a stage. He flushed with shame as he remembered Mrs. Pinn's remark: They say, Mr. Erlich, that Raizel is relieving Mrs. Erlich of many of her duties. That's real family feeling for you. It was true. Raizel had done a lot for Sheinka. She had brought Ruth back from hospital after her operation; she was taking her to school on Monday; she ran errands for Sheinka. Why then should his body burn with shame when he recalled that sharp-nosed witch's words?

He and Raizel had nothing to hide. For years they had walked home together, occasionally with Berka, often with Leib Schwartzman, sometimes by themselves. On those occasions he had joked with Mrs. Zlotnik while she watered her potted geraniums; exchanged greetings with old Weinbrin who was reading 'Der Yiddisher Americaner' over the top of his glasses; enquired after Tova Perlman's son who had bought a business on the East Rand, or stopped to admire that crazy Mrs. Hirshman's cats.

Tonight, suddenly, the friendly arc of conversation which had flowed from one side of the street to the other, seemed like a menacing passageway through which he had to walk warily, expecting barbed remarks instead of warm words. He grunted a greeting to Mrs. Zlotnik, ignored Mrs. Hirshman's cats and barely said hello to old Weinbrin.

They walked past a group of children who were playing 'Oranges and Lemons', a game which he had never understood. He wondered at their squeals of fear as they ran through the arch formed by two children. He wondered at his own anxieties and guilts. The senseless games people played.

'Hey, Dovidke, why do you look so fierce?' Shmuel the plumber called out as they went past his house. 'Has Sheinkala presented you with yet another daughter?'

Dovid threw him such an angry look that Shmuel was surprised into silence.

Raizel walked calmly beside him, returning everyone's greetings, asking after their health, holding back her tears. The four blocks' walk seemed endless to Dovid. When they reached Berka's house, in silence, he said goodbye brusquely and was about to walk on when Berka came out of the house.

'Dovid, Ruthie's here. She's in trouble with Sheinka and won't go home without you.'

Dovid turned back reluctantly and went into the house.

4

When Ruth saw Dovid's stern, withdrawn face she began to cry again.

'I'll bring her home later,' Berka said as he led Dovid out of the room. 'And tell Sheinka to act like a mensch. She scares the life out of Ruth with her threats and wails.'

'So, my maidala,' he said, putting Ruth onto his lap again. 'Where were we up to?'

'The man was walking in the veld,' Ruth said wiping her nose with the back of her hand, 'there, behind the plantation, and he tripped over a stone and it was made of gold. Did he turn into a prince?'

'No. Poor old George just disappeared off the scene and died without a penny to his name. The rich men came up from the diamond diggings in Kimberley and found gold near the rock he had tripped over. And that's how the mines began.'

'He was a schlemiel, like Zeide Berchik,' Yenta said as she came into the lounge. 'Your Zeide could've bought up half of Mayfontein in the early days, for next to nothing. But who wants property? Others bought. Today they're rich and he's still mending their boots.'

'Mrs. Grimm, your fairy tales I don't need in my business,' Berka said.

'Does the child need them? Sheinka's right. You're driving her mad with all your stories.'

'Your tzimmes is burning,' Berka said sniffing the air with exaggerated concern.

Yenta fled to the kitchen.

'My father says it's all ugly, the dumps, the veld, the dam.

He wants to go back to Ragaza where there's snow in winter and rivers and where wild strawberries grow in the woods.'

'That's where he was born. You were born here. Do you think the dumps are ugly?'

'No, but mamma shouts when I go there. And she says a little kaffir boy sank into the slimes dam one day and they never found him again. He was also sliding down the dumps on a piece of iron.'

'That's dangerous. You shouldn't go there alone. I'll take you one Sunday, any Sunday. Remember when we walked in the veld and picked those lovely kosmos?'

'I remember. Zeide Berchik,' she asked shyly, 'am I ugly?'

'What a ridiculous idea!'

'But am I?' she persisted, dusting particles of sand off her leg. She turned away, afraid of his verdict.

'Certainly not! You're going to be as tall and as straight as a young bluegum; you've got cheeks like red apples and the loveliest green eyes I've ever seen. And I've seen plenty.'

'Mamma says I look like my other zeide, Red Yehuda.'

'He was a fine figure of a man, Yehuda was.'

'Mamma says he had ugly red hair. She doesn't like red hair. She says the baby is going to have black hair, like hers.'

'Your father's got red hair.'

'She doesn't like him either.'

'Ruthie! You musn't say such things.'

'It's true, Zeide Berchik. I heard her tell him so one night when they thought I was asleep.'

Berka lifted her up and kissed her. Zutzke ran eagerly at their heels as they walked out of the house.

'Your mother's not well at the moment but after the baby is born everything will be all right again. Be patient and good and listen to her. On Monday you're going to school with that nice case and crayons Raizel bought you. You'll make friends and soon you'll be playing "Oranges and Lemons" with those children down the street.'

'I don't like them. They pull my hair and tease me when I speak.'

'You'll speak English better than they do one day, you'll see.'

Where would my Yenta rest her bosom, Berka speculated

as he walked onto Sheinka's highly polished red veranda where little pots of geraniums stood all along the ledge, screening it from the street. To accommodate Yenta's ample bosom she'd have to remove half the pots.

The front door stood open and the smell of carbolic soap, boiled chicken and cinnamon buns drifted out towards them. The lace curtains, skilfully darned in places, were white and starched. The linoleum which ran down the length of the passage gleamed.

Dovid and Sheinka were sitting in the lounge. It was obvious that there had been angry words between them.

'My child!' Sheinka swooped down on Ruth who stood very still, allowing herself to be embraced. 'Come. Let us sit on the sofa and look through the photo album together. But first,' she said looking at the sand on Ruth's arms and legs, 'we'll have to wash.'

Ruth followed her meekly out of the lounge. She loved the photo album which was locked in the sideboard next to the wine and sweets. She knew the inmates of the album better than she knew the people in Mayfontein: the members of the choir who picnicked on the banks of the river; Sheinka's girl-hood friends; aunts and uncles whom she had seen on Yenta's walls; snow in the streets of Ragaza; and all those pictures of Sheinka where she looked so young and pretty, and not at all cross.

Sheinka always sighed when she brushed off an imaginary speck of dust from the forehead of a dark young man who held a violin under his chin.

'He might have been your father,' she told Ruth with a fine disregard for biological fact, 'but his mother interfered. Much joy she had from the match she forced on him,' she added bitterly each time she told the story. 'The girl was rich and ugly and kicked her mother-in-law out of her house after the marriage. Shimon vowed never to play the violin again after we parted, and I promised never to sing again.'

These reminiscences were usually followed by a recital of sad love songs which apparently did not constitute a breach of that vow.

Looking through the album lulled Sheinka into a calm but melancholy mood and Ruth knew that she was safe from nagging or reprimand during this period. Sheinka might even put her arms around Ruth and address her as 'my poor child', Ruth never knew why.

'Where's Gittel?' Berka asked, satisfied that a temporary peace had been established between mother and child. 'I want to wish her a good sabbath.'

'In the kitchen,' Dovid replied picking up the 'Forwerts'. He lifted the paper close to his face, shutting himself off from further conversation. Berka shrugged and walked into the kitchen.

A snowy cloth covered the deal kitchen table. On one side lay a sheet of thinly rolled noodle dough. At the other end stood Gittel, a white scarf thrown over her head, her hands covering her face, blessing the sabbath candles.

'Blessed art thou, O Lord our God, King of the Universe, who has hallowed us by His Commandments and commanded us to kindle the sabbath light,' she murmured rapidly in Hebrew. Then she sighed, and keeping her hands over her face, added a private prayer in Yiddish.

'God in Heaven, I don't ask for happiness or riches. All I want is that you should send me a little nachas, a little joy, from my children. What wrongs have I committed that I should have a son in a distant land who has forgotten his mother? He hasn't written her a single line in two years. I keep a kosher home, I guard the sabbath, I read your holy books even if they are in Yiddish translation. You know how it was in der heim. We women weren't taught to read Hebrew. You've seen how I kasher the dishes and cutlery for Pesach, how I stick the cutlery into the ground and how I soak the dishes in boiling water into which I throw hot coals. I go to shul on shabbas and on all the Festivals and I help the poor when I've got with what. Why then, God in Heaven, should you not grant me a little nachas from my children?

'I don't complain that I'm dependent on a bad-tempered daughter (forgive her, God, she has her own troubles), or that I have to take charity from a reluctant son-in-law. It is better than taking from strangers, though sometimes I wonder. I'm thankful that I've got my own bed — during the War seven of us slept side by side in my mother's bed — even if it does stand in the dining-room. I'm thankful also that I have enough

47

to eat though you may have noticed that I never touch chicken or other delicacies: I don't want to be a burden, an expense to Dovid. Anyway, I survive. But if it is indeed your will that I should continue to survive, Lord, I ask you only one thing: a little nachas from my children . . .'

Berka backed away quietly when he saw the tears run down onto the front of Gittel's dress through her fingers. He felt guilty about eavesdropping on her conversation with God, no friend of his. Gittel was the only person he knew who made God seem a possibility.

He passed by the bathroom where he heard Ruth splashing about, into the lounge where Dovid sat, half-concealed by the newspaper.

'Have you written to your mother lately?' Berka asked.

'My mother?' Dovid sat up, letting the paper fall into his lap. 'Since when do you keep a check on my correspondence with my mother?'

'Don't get excited. I only asked. One would think I was prying into your love life. In a moment of weakness you confided that you didn't write regularly because you couldn't send money. If you need . . .'

'If I need I'll ask, thank you,' Dovid said gruffly picking up the newspaper again.

'Gut shabbas, Berka. I thought I heard your voice,' Gittel said from the doorway. She had taken off her white scarf and was smoothing down her wispy grey hair. She fingered the front of her dress, trying to eradicate the trace of tears.

'Gut shabbas, Gittel. I just came to say hello. I haven't seen you all week. Listen, I have a plan,' he said going into the passage with her. 'Yenta wants to go to bioscope tomorrow evening. You're coming with us this time and I'm not taking no for an answer.'

'You and Yenta go in good health and enjoy yourselves,' she said resignedly. 'What do you want to schlepp along an old woman for? I've lived without bioscope for over sixty years and I'll survive without it. Tonight I fetch "Der Yiddisher Americaner" from Mr. Weinbrin and I'll have plenty to read and keep me occupied.'

Berka smiled. The Yiddish newspaper was Gittel's only contact with the outside world. She read the news section avidly and often discussed two-month-old events with him as though they were burning topical issues. She also followed a serialised love story called 'The Dark Stranger'. She borrowed a line from the heroine which she used whenever she looked tear-stained: 'I've been peeling onions,' she would quote solemnly. Her favourite column, however, was written by a Miss Breen, the lonely hearts expert, who was her oracle.

'I'll fetch you tomorrow evening at eight,' Berka said firmly. 'Wear your nice blue dress. It suits you.'

'Berka,' she said at the gate. 'I know you've got good reason for disliking Benjamin. Yes, yes. Yenta told me long ago that you signed security for him that time he bought a grocery shop and that you had to pay out a lot of money when he made himself bankrupt, mechula. He's not a clever man and perhaps not even an honest one, although he is a bit of a rabbi. But he's getting old, his sight is failing and he's sick. You're such a kind man, Berka. Make allowance for him once more. It'll make things easier for Yenta.'

Berka looked into her large brown eyes which were filling with tears again. She reminded him of Ruth. He hoped that Ruth would not peel as many onions as her grandmother.

'All right,' he kissed her finely-creased forehead. 'I'll keep out of his way. But don't ask me to love him.'

God is one. What a fallacy, Berka mused as he walked past Mrs. Zaidman's house through whose open window he saw the sabbath candles wavering in the soft evening air. Everyone had his private god: Gittel, Hershl, Dovid, even Ruthie. Gittel's was a domestic god. He sat in his celestial lounge watching benignly as his female worshippers threw hot coals in among the soaking everyday dishes, making them ritually acceptable for the Passover. He beamed with delight when Gittel wrenched the meat dishcloth out of the black servant's hands just as she was about to dry the milk jug with it; 'Chaim Leib is to write to his mother, she's due for a little nachas,' he thundered when she salted the meat according to the law, allowing the blood to drain before she cooked it. And he assigned her a place in Heaven when she put on her old black hat, clasped her tattered prayer book to her breast and hurried to shul, walking quickly towards it, as custom prescribed, and slowly away from it, savouring the holiness she had imbibed in that musty old building.

Gittel was probably right to site God in a celestial lounge: He was certainly not in Spain, nor in Nazi Germany, nor for that matter, was he an observer at the Moscow trials.

The candles in Hershl's house were also sending up blue flames to heaven. Hershl's God was temporarily in exile and had to be consoled with traditional practices and prayers until the day when he would sit on a secular throne in Palestine. And Dovid, his befuddled but beloved Dovid, had an elusive god who would not show his face to mankind until man himself had restored peace and justice on earth.

Berka walked to the corner of First Avenue and Twelfth Street. The synagogue was a block away. The first worshippers had already come out of shul and were being followed by groups of others who fanned out in all directions towards their homes where a typical sabbath dinner awaited them. After they had said a blessing over the wine and the sabbath kitke, they would be served a portion of gefilte fish which would be eaten with horseradish or mustard. At home Berka chose to eat the minced horseradish: Yenta's mustard looked like congealed ear wax. Chicken soup with finely cut lokshen would be served next, and the main course was the inevitable chicken which had already provided the flavour of the soup, with stuffing or tzimmes at the side. On summer evenings the family would sit on the stoep at the end of the meal and sip hot lemon tea through a lump of hard sugar, and in winter they would gather around the kitchen stove.

Berka shook himself out of his mellowing mood. I'd give a prize to the woman who had the nerve to serve up fish and chips from Davis's shop on a Friday night, he thought. Slaves, that's all they are; slaves to habit and tradition.

Echoes of discussions and arguments filtered down through the still summer's air towards Berka as he stood on the corner in his working clothes, as solitary as the evening star which was rising in a deep purple sky.

5

*T*he service had already begun when Hershl slipped into his seat, followed by Daniel his youngest son. He nodded across the aisle to Leib Schwartzman whose sonorous voice rang through the synagogue, welcoming the sabbath:

> 'Come, Oh Cherished one, and meet the Bride!
> Let us welcome the face of sabbath . . .'

He found the place in the prayer book for Daniel who watched the congregants carefully and turned the pages when they did. Hershl, in the meantime, joined in the prayers. The synagogue was fairly full but there were few women in the gallery. Tomorrow morning they would come but tonight they were at home, blessing the candles, preparing the sabbath meal. It was hot and stuffy in the synagogue in spite of the open windows, and the cheder boys in the back seats were restive and noisy. The shammas moved menacingly among them, delivering a corrective blow here and there in a practised, absent-minded manner without interrupting his prayers.

Facing the Ark, in the place of honour, sat Uncle Feldman flanked by Isaac Kowarsky and Avram Segal. The latter two had earned their places through piety and learning. Uncle Feldman, after considerable pressure from the Committee, had given a large donation on his seventieth birthday. He had remained a member of the Mayfontein Congregation because here, he confided to Hershl, he was ensured a place of honour. In Houghton, he spat out the name of his suburb with contempt, those newly-rich Jews did not appreciate a man of his calibre.

Hershl watched the old man fumble his way through the service. His chauffeur parked the car half-way up the block and Uncle Feldman came into the shul with the breathless air of a man who had walked ten miles. He was old, Hershl conceded, but he certainly displayed more energy in his Concession Store. Only last week Hershl had seen him sprint across the dusty floor like an eighteen-year-old, to check on the amount his harassed manager had rung up on the till.

And there, behind Leib who was singing like an angel, sat the Reverend Benjamin, back in town after a long absence. Yenta knew only part of the reason for Berka's dislike for Benjamin. He never told her about Benjamin's liaison with a Boer woman in the diggings which had resulted in a progeny of several daughters, all of whom Benjamin had finally abandoned. It would be disastrous, Benjamin had protested when Berka urged him to marry the woman, for a man of his religious calling to form a permanent association with a goya.

Benjamin had grown fatter and blinder since Hershl had last seen him. His short neck had disappeared behind several chins which trembled with piety as he sang a hymn to Queen Sabbath. He lifted his thick-lensed glasses in the direction of Heaven and prayed with abandon.

Hershl could not give himself to the service that evening. It took time to unwind. He had rushed home from work, climbed into the steaming bath which Faigel had prepared for him but had hardly begun to relax when she reappeared with his clean underwear and sabbath suit, urging him to get to shul on time. The transition from the working week to the sabbath had always been preceded by a rush, especially in the old country.

'In Bod arein! In Bod arein! Yidden, in Bod arein!' the shammas had called through the streets of his home town, summoning the Jews to the bathhouse before the sabbath. Thin men, fat men, young boys, old men, all rushed through the streets, trailing their clean clothing. Everyone slapped himself with brooms of supple aromatic twigs in the steamy atmosphere of the public bath, laughing, shouting, arguing. Privacy was an acquired taste, Hershl had decided in his bath earlier that evening, to which one finally became addicted. But he had loved the bathhouse atmosphere, the sense of community.

How different it was in his little bathroom where the steam

fogged up the mirror and where the only sound was the drip, drip, drip of the leaking tap into a bathful of water. Here a man could think, plan or relax, according to his mood. There one had been caught up bodily, spiritually, into a swirl of naked humanity and was carried into the life of every other individual. Could one feel distant from a man when one knew he had a brown birthmark on his buttocks?

Pardon the vulgar expression, Hershl apologised to the domed ceiling.

He felt a keen sense of loss when he thought about the bathhouse. Privacy had its price. He understood what Dovid meant when he said that he felt out of joint in South Africa, as though he were hanging on the edge of a continent, at the end of the world. Everything was upside down. One celebrated Passover, a spring festival, in autumn, and Shavuoth, the harvest festival, in spring. In der heim the Ark had been built into the east wall of the synagogue, facing the Temple's site in Jerusalem. Here it was built into the north wall. But the difference was not merely one of geography or of season. Something invaluable had been lost. It was only at shul these days or at a wedding or a barmitzvah that Hershl met with all his old friends and experienced this sense of community.

In Palestine it would be restored and there, please God, it would exist on a higher and more meaningful level.

'Next year in Jerusalem,' he prayed out of context.

The short Friday night service was over. Hershl shook hands with Rabbi Josselson and was walking out when he found himself behind the Reverend Benjamin and Uncle Feldman.

'And how's that wild Boer, my nephew?' Uncle Feldman asked Benjamin.

'Now, now, Reb Feldman,' Benjamin said, 'Berka's not a bad chap. A little hasty perhaps, obstinate, a poor provider, an out-and-out atheist, but a bad chap he's not. If he were he wouldn't have produced such delightful children, the evil eye shouldn't harm them. You've met them, of course?'

'Once. When they were small,' Uncle Feldman said brusquely.

'The girl's a beauty and the boy's a chemist. Or nearly a chemist. He writes his final exams at the end of this year. Works

53

all day and studies all night. So intelligent that he could turn his hand to anything. It's a pity . . .'

'Yes, yes, it's a pity,' Uncle Feldman said crossly. 'It's a pity he's got an ox for a father. Ruined his chances and those of his children. Rich they could've been. Of course I'm interested in them. My trouble is that I'm too soft and forgiving. Listen Benjamin,' he said drawing closer. 'It's difficult to find honest, intelligent employees. If the boy has more sense than his father, tell him to contact me. We've just bought a bankrupt drygoods firm. If he's as intelligent as you say he is . . .'

Hershl turned away hastily. He had already heard too much. He prayed that for once in his life Benjamin would have the good sense to mind his own business and not pass the message on to Joel.

Hershl took Daniel's hand while they waited for his two older sons, Joshua and Moshe. They had been among the noisy boys at the back of the shul and Hershl hoped that one or two of the shammas's blows had landed on them. He himself never laid a hand on his sons, but there were times . . .

The noise and the heat had been oppressive. It was refreshing to stand in the cool evening breeze without a ceiling between himself and God. Hershl smiled up at the dark velvety sky. It was a reflection of life on earth: stars like sugar crystals, a moon like half a beigel.

'Gut shabbes tatteh,' the boys said as they shook hands with Hershl and kissed him on the cheek. Joshua or Jossie as he was called at home, was nine and Moshe eleven. Good boys. Hershl's eyes filled with tears of gladness as he walked away from the synagogue. A little wild at times but independent, truthful and healthy, thank God.

Until recently Faigel had worked in the bakery all day. The boys, when they returned from school, took their lunch from the ice box or from the oven, changed out of school uniform, then ran off to cheder. Faigel had taken Daniel to kindergarten on her way to work and brought him to the bakery at lunch time. He was a lonely boy, Hershl thought giving his hand a warm squeeze. He spent the afternoons on the bakery floor, moulding horses and oxen out of pieces of dough. At school, Hershl hoped, he would make friends.

The smell of sabbath cooking drifted through the dimly-lit streets and Hershl increased his pace. He neither loved nor hated Mayfontein as Berka and Dovid did. For him it was a place to live in. His family was there, his friends, his business. What did it matter that the mine machinery roared and crunched its way through the night; that the little verandas were always covered with mine dust; that the mosquitoes bred profusely in the smelly dam at the foot of the dumps? What was important was the environment that man created within himself. He would, of course, have preferred to nurture this inner environment in Palestine, but until he went there it mattered little to him where he lived. To Faigel, unfortunately, it mattered a great deal.

The local high school only went up to Standard Eight. This, he supposed, was sufficient for the miners' sons who would follow their fathers into the mines. He, however, had other plans for his sons. They would study. The nearest high school to which both Joel and Raizel had gone, was two trams and forty minutes away from Mayfontein. 'Either one of us travels, or three of us will have to,' Faigel said pointedly.

It looked as though one of them would travel. But that was still in the future and Hershl refused to think about it. By the time the boys went to high school, God willing, he would buy a car and travelling would not be a problem.

He liked Mayfontein best at night when the outlines of the cramped little houses merged with the dark and when the dusty dumps on the edge of the suburb vanished from sight. Only a delicate row of lights was visible, running from the base to the top of the dump, outlining the course of the coco-pan rail. He loved to walk down the dark sand roads and look into the lit-up houses where each family lived with its own parcel of joy and sorrow.

Tonight the sabbath candles burned away in every Jewish home, even in Berka's, despite his protests. All over the world they were burning. But not in Germany, not in Germany. Or if they were, they burned in secrecy and in fear. God alone knew what was happening there.

Rebainu Shelailem, he appealed to the sugar-frosted sky, take care of your children. Shield them from the Nazi horror.

He entered his house in a chastened mood. He hung his hat on the hallstand, washed his hands and went into the dining-room. Above the sideboard was a picture of a man with a dark bushy beard and fine prophetic eyes. After God, Theodore Herzl. Berka disputed the order but then neither God nor the father of Zionism figured in Berka's pantheon of gods, if he had one. Hershl lowered his eyes before the picture, put on his yarmulka and said a blessing over a goblet of wine. Silver candlesticks stood in the centre of the table, and the melting wax dripped down the sides of the candles like molten tears. Even a stone would cry for the misfortunes of his people.

'The sabbath is a time for rejoicing,' Hershl said shaking off his dark mood. 'Faigel, the fish is excellent.'

'Too much saffron, too little salt,' she replied reluctant as ever to accept a compliment.

But try not giving one, Hershl thought. She would bristle with farible, with a grievance, for a week. A fine woman, Faigel, but as sensitive as a hair in the wind. Such, he supposed, were the ways of women although he did not consider himself an authority on the subject. An excellent wife and mother to be sure, but as much a mystery today as she had been when he first met her.

She was a baker's daughter, a quiet, dark-haired girl to whom he had become increasingly attached when he visited their home during his lonely years as a Torah student in Vilna. He had originally been attracted to her vivacious younger sister but before he realised what was happening he had proposed to Faigel. He suspected some quiet campaigning in the background but so subtle had it been, if it had in fact been, that he was never sure of it.

When they arrived in South Africa it was she who suggested opening a bakery. He could not support a family on his earnings as a Hebrew teacher. She performed tasks both menial and delicate, from kneading dough and stoking the ovens to decorating cakes. If she was a little tight with money today, one could forgive her: she had worked hard to earn it.

'The lokshen pudding melts in the mouth,' he said, returning his plate for a second helping.

'Too crisp at the corners,' she replied. 'Eat, Moishala, eat. It's all bones,' she said piling another helping of boiled chicken

56

onto his plate. Daniel was still toying with his first helping.

'Who, in der heim,' Hershl said pushing away his empty plate, 'was sure of having a chicken for the sabbath? Do you know, children, when a poor man ate chicken? Either when he was sick or when the chicken was. We are very fortunate to be so well off and healthy. But we must never forget others who are less fortunate.'

'You don't,' Faigel said sharply. 'You give away half your earnings.'

'Don't exaggerate, Faigala. I give away only a small portion. I wish I had more to give.'

'Tatteh,' Daniel said. 'When you say we must think of others, do you mean the shocherdikke as well?'

'Kaffirs, my child, kaffirs. Schocherdikke isn't a nice word,' Hershl corrected gently. 'Of course. They're men, not beasts. Why do you ask?'

'Because today a shoch... a kaffir fell off his bicycle near the bakery and he lay on the ground bleeding and nobody helped him until the ambulance came. They said he was drunk.'

'Oy vey, talk of happier things,' Faigel interrupted. 'Blood and schocherdikke. It's enough to make one's meal curdle in the stomach. Come. Let's have our tea on the veranda.'

'Leave the lights off,' Hershl said as Faigel reached for the switch. 'If the mosquitoes want a meal let them look for it in the dark. For that alone I wish the summer was over already.'

On his darkened veranda Hershl felt as though he was in a theatre. The stage, the street; the setting, the lit-up verandas; the performers, his neighbours; the play, plotless, nameless, changing with circumstance but retaining the repetitive rhythm of a religious ritual. On Friday nights children gathered from all over the neighbourhood to play bok-bok, kicking the milk tin, and other queerly-named games. His own sons watched enviously as the others leapt onto one another's backs or ran through the streets kicking a tin with stones in it. On Fridays the goyim had the run of the street. The Jewish boys, against their inclination, were restrained from running wild. It was sabbath.

Tomorrow night they would join in the games.

Dovid and Sheinka sat in silence on their veranda, he with

his 'Forwerts', the Jewish labour paper from America, and she staring mournfully into the dark sky, her head to one side as though she was listening to music. Leib was sitting on his chair with his legs raised onto the ledge, his hands linked behind his head, humming the melodies from the Friday night service.

Gittel walked up to Yenta's house and stood talking to her and Benjamin, an occasional performer who played the villain's role. It was a pity that Benjamin's presence on the stage precluded Berka's, by far Hershl's favourite character.

Hershl leaned back and closed his eyes. He was drowsy. The play would continue without him; he needed a nap.

From the date palms and olive trees he knew that he was in Palestine, but instead of Arabs on camels, he saw a column of black-coated men goose-stepping over the sand dunes, shouting 'Heil Hitler!' He himself was standing next to a well and although he knew that he should hide, run away or wake up, he could not act. As they drew nearer he roused himself and tried to run but his legs would not move.

He tore himself out of the dream to find his face pouring with sweat. Everything looked strange and distant. He looked over at the divided house which Berka shared with Burger and a shudder ran through him. Both verandas were lit up. Burger sat on one with his son and Berka was on the other, talking to Raizel. A strange heaviness weighed on Hershl's heart.

'I'm tired,' he said to Faigel, 'and have been haunted by strange thoughts all evening. Perhaps I ate too much of your excellent kugel. What I really need is a good sleep.'

He kissed her on the forehead as he went inside, unable to shake off his dark thoughts.

6

*A*fter Sheinka switched off the light Ruth lay stiffly in bed, waiting anxiously for the heavy black forms around her to take on their natural shapes again: the high-backed bed in which her grandmother slept; the chest of drawers; the table in the centre of the room surrounded by wooden chairs. The curtains were drawn but as the breeze blew them gently inwards, Ruth saw a strip of star-lit sky.

Her grandmother had gone to visit Uncle Benjamin, and her parents were in the lounge, arguing in muted tones.

'I tell you the child's asleep. With that mangy dog at her feet. I'll get rid of him one day, that filthy beast. Besides, she doesn't understand,' Sheinka was saying.

Ruth sat up and clasped Zutzke protectively to her chest.

'It's enough already,' she heard her father say wearily. 'I've heard it all before and I tell you it's nonsense.'

'It's true! It's true! I've seen how you look at her. She's always hanging around our house.'

'Doing things for you,' Dovid said angrily. 'You send her around like a servant girl.'

'She offers. Not to help me; to impress you. And she has. You've always had a soft spot for teachers. First Russian teachers, now English teachers. But I'll kick her out, I'll make a row, I'll shout it from the rooftops . . .' Sheinka's voice rose hysterically.

'Quiet, quiet!' Dovid commanded in a tone Ruth had never heard from him. There was a shuffling of feet.

'You hit me!' Sheinka cried out.

Ruth put her hands over her ears.

'Make them stop, God,' she appealed to the strips of sky through the curtains. 'Please make them stop.'

She took her hands away from her ears and heard only the roar of the stamp mills, the chugging of a train in the distance, and the crickets in the veld. Zutzke snored contentedly at her feet. When she shut her eyes she saw men on horses, blood in snowy streets and houses burning. She opened them wide and stared into the dark until the images dissolved. Then she thought of the golden mine dumps and the faces in the photo album. Her mother had held her close as she turned the pages and Ruth felt the baby's jerky movements in her belly.

'He wants to come out,' she whispered. 'He can't breathe in there.'

Ruth turned restlessly in her bed. Kkrr-um, kkrrr-um, the crushers roared. She began to breathe in unison with the thunderous crashes, heavily, unevenly. What would happen if she stopped breathing, just for minute? She was tired of breathing. Would she die? A feeling of panic rose up from her stomach towards her throat, constricting it with fear. If the crushers stopped working, would she stop breathing? As she breathed more rapidly, her hands and legs went into a cramp. How did the baby breathe in the stomach? How could the miners breathe inside the earth? A black mask moved towards her in the dark and an unseen hand clamped it over her nose and mouth. She leapt from bed crying:

'I can't breathe! I can't breathe!'

Dovid ran into the room. He lifted her out of bed and took her to the open window, pulling apart the curtains. He stood there until her breathing slowed down, then put her back to bed. Zutzke was whining in a corner.

'Sing me a song, tatteh,' she said holding on to his hand.

'Not tonight, child. Sleep now.'

He waited until she had settled down, then tiptoed out of the room. She turned over onto her back and moved her hand slowly over her flat stomach, down towards her thighs. As she glided over the soft rises and slipped into dark, petalled crevices, visions of golden sand floated through her mind. She reached the innermost core, smoothed it gently towards the warm silky sands, into it, through it, around it, until she was submerged in a rush of warmth and delight which left her limp and tranquil.

When Dovid returned to the lounge, Sheinka had gone. Never before had he raised a hand to her. He held it away from his body as though it were a filthy thing. He found her in the bedroom, packing.

'Call a taxi,' she said heavily. 'The pains have started.'

The Matron did not allow him to remain at the maternity home. She promised to phone when the baby was born. Dovid spent the night in the lounge, drinking the coffee which Gittel urged on him from time to time. She herself lay awake on her soft feather bed while Ruth tossed about restlessly, moaning in her sleep. The night noises of Mayfontein did not disturb Gittel. They were muted by the perpetual buzzing in her ears which Brown the pharmacist had diagnosed as high blood pressure. He gave her a strong peppermint-flavoured mixture which upset her gallstones but did not alleviate the buzzing.

The call from the maternity home came through at five o'clock in the morning.

'It's a boy, they're both well, he weighs eight pounds two ounces,' Dovid repeated to Gittel before he closed himself in his room and fell into a heavy dreamless sleep.

The neighbours called early to wish Gittel and Dovid 'Mazeltov'. She was somber, he was red-eyed. Hershl kissed Dovid on both cheeks.

'Have lots of nachas from your son,' he said.

'The ranks of the working class are expanding,' Leib beamed, patting Dovid on the shoulder.

Berka embraced Dovid wordlessly, then walked out of the house with Gittel. She was wearing her black hat and was on her way to the synagogue to say a blessing for the new-born baby.

'Don't forget,' he said leaving her outside the synagogue, 'We're going to bioscope tonight. This is an occasion for celebration.'

Raizel stood in the kitchen, watching Yenta make taiglach for the bris, the circumcision ceremony.

'From two and two to five and three,' Yenta said. 'My dreams are becoming less reliable. I'll have to work out another system. Mrs. Zlotnik writes out all the numbers on a piece of paper, takes a pen, closes her eyes . . .'

'I'd better wish Dovid mazeltov,' Raizel said.

When she left, Yenta closed the window — draughts were bad for taiglach; locked the front door — Faigel's yeast buns had fallen flat when Mrs. Pinn unexpectedly walked in while she was baking, and sighed heavily as she watched the doughy O's toss about in the boiling syrup. She should have been making taiglach for Raizel's wedding. Next birthday she would be twenty-two and there was still no sign of a husband.

Dovid was on his way to the nursing home when Raizel arrived. She stifled a feeling of utter desolation as she shook his limp hand. There was a newcomer in his world, the world into which she had not even established a foothold. Ruth ran up and put both arms around Raizel's neck.

'I didn't even want a brother,' she confided.

Visiting hours were from ten to eleven. Dovid walked slowly up to the tram stop and watched the Saturday morning crowd mill through the streets. The miners' wives with their shopping baskets; Jews in their sabbath best; children freed from a week's school queueing outside the Roxy to see 'The Masked Rider' with Tom Mix. Poorly-dressed black men stepped off the pavement before the shoppers and waited patiently at the back of shops until the white people had been served. A strange race, black as pitch. Dovid did not understand or like them, but his heart ached at the stripping of human dignity.

Perhaps he should bring Sheinka some fruit. He would catch a tram further down the road, he thought as he walked towards Chidrawi's shop. It required an effort not to look into Nathan's Drapery Store.

'Give me half a dozen yellow cling peaches,' he said absent-mindedly to Chidrawi. 'And a pound of grapes,' he added, remembering that Sheinka did not like peaches.

He ran across the road in time to catch the approaching tram. It was crammed with dressed up women going into town. Mrs. Nathan was among them. She nodded to Dovid in a queenly manner and made no comment on the birth of his son, a calculated piece of indifference for which Dovid felt grateful. Mrs. Nathan affected to know nothing of what went on in the suburb. Fashion was her world.

The tram thundered down the Dip, past Berka's shop where Dovid caught a glimpse of him in his leather apron, with nails between his pursed lips, bent over the last. And there, beyond the Dip lay Berka's fabulous city of gold. Sodom and Gomorrah. An ugly city with dull grey structures crowding over narrow streets.

At Market Square he caught another tram which took him up Hospital Hill to the maternity home. At the terminus he went into the large pharmacy where Joel worked. Sheinka, on the way to the hospital last night, had asked him to bring her another jar of Vicks.

Joel stood behind the counter in a short white coat with a high collar. His resemblance to Raizel is uncanny, Dovid thought while he waited for Joel to wrap a parcel for a customer. But there was a cold edge to his smile and his eyes glinted with professional politeness as he inclined his head slightly to the customer. Dovid did not see much of Joel whose free time was spent with his rich friends.

'Congratulations on the birth of your son, David,' Joel said in English. He was the only one who called him David. 'My mother told me the grand news this morning. All well?'

'Thank you,' Dovid said gruffly. 'One medium bottle of Vicks please.'

Cold fish. To see the same eyes, the same mouth, all without life or warmth. Her eyes . . . My God, he thought in desperation. Is there no escape from this obsession?

There were five other women in the ward with Sheinka. She was lying back on the pillows, pale, with dark rings under her eyes. She began to cry when Dovid sat down beside her.

'I said terrible things last night, Dovid,' she began. 'But it was my uncertainty, my fear talking, not me. You've been so distant lately.'

'I'm sorry I raised my hand to you, Sheinka,' he answered staring down at the pattern on the bed cover. 'And at such a time.'

'If only you would speak to me more. You've been such a stranger.'

'Shah, shah. Don't upset yourself. Let's talk of other things. How's the baby?'

'All rumpled and red like new-born babies are. But Dovid, it's true. You never speak to me.'

'I try, Sheinka, but as soon as I come home you begin to complain about your piles, about the blood you spit up, about your senna pods. What can I say that will match this morbid interest you have in your health?'

'You see, you don't believe that I'm sick.' She began to cry again.

'Sheinka,' Dovid patted her arm, 'This is not the time for tears. Tell me more about the . . . our baby.'

'He's big and healthy the doctor said. And he's got lots of black hair. Maybe that's why I had such heartburn . . .' She broke off abruptly.

They were silent for a while, then she started to cry.

'What is it, Sheinka?' he asked fighting down his irritation.

'The nurses took away my Vicks. If they find the new bottle they'll take that too. Hide it, Dovid. And tell them I must have it because of my weak lungs. I can't explain in English.'

At that moment a robust woman in white marched into the ward. She came across to Sheinka's bed.

'Mr. Erlich? Good. Perhaps you'll understand. Your wife has the unfortunate habit of rubbing Vicks into her chest as you no doubt know. She's a big healthy girl and doesn't need it. She'll be able to breast feed for months and months, but if she persists in using Vicks she'll suffocate the poor mite. Try to dissuade her from using it. I assure you she'll survive.'

Dovid sat out the whole visit persuading Sheinka not to fret over the loss of her Vicks.

'Goodbye,' he said bending over and kissing her on the forehead. 'I'm not coming back tonight because Gittel is going to bioscope with Berka and Yenta. Ruth'll be alone.'

'Dovid,' she said hesitantly. 'Dovid, promise me one thing.'

He waited apprehensively as she blew her nose loudly.

'Anything reasonable,' he said cautiously.

'Give up your English lessons,' she said. 'And I'll change. I'll . . . I'll try to be well, as well as it is possible for me to be. I know how my illnesses irritate you.'

All expression left his face. He looked down at her pale bloated face on which two red patches had appeared over the cheekbones.

'It's not important to me,' he said quietly. 'If you want it so badly, I'll have no more English lessons.'

By the time he came home he felt drained, as though he had given birth to the baby. He found Ruth sitting among the crushed stones in the garden, examining them with great interest.

'Have you lost something, Ruthie?'

'No, I'm looking for something.' She glanced up at him and asked gravely. 'What colour hair has the baby got?'

She looked thoughtful when he answered, 'Black'.

'What are you looking for, Ruth?'

'Gold,' she replied putting a stone into a brown paper bag. 'Zeide Berchik says these stones come from the mine. I've already found some with gold that they forgot to take out.'

Dovid leaned over and stroked her hair.

'And what are you going to do with the gold?'

'I'll give some to Bobbe Yenta to buy a chemist shop for Joel, and some to Bobbe Gittel for rent, and some to you to send my Bobbe in Ragaza. And with the rest I'll buy lots of pink ice cream from Mr. Schumacher.'

Dovid kissed her. Fool's gold had become an invaluable metal. And only last night Sheinka had said that the child did not understand.

7

When Berka looked out of his bedroom window towards dusk he saw Benjamin pacing the pavement. Now and again he would peer into the sky, then resume his ungainly vigil.

'What's that lunatic doing?' he asked Yenta. 'Praying?'

'He's waiting for the first star that will end the sabbath,' she laughed. 'He wants a cigarette.'

'The holy man,' Berka said. 'Have you been outside to the lavatory today? It's full of cigarette butts and smoke. Raizel doesn't smoke, Joel doesn't smoke and I smoke a pipe. Holy man,' he repeated, pulling on his best trousers.

Yenta felt affectionate towards Berka. When Benjamin had come in from shul the previous evening Berka had greeted him, gruffly, it must be said, but he had greeted him. When he mentioned casually that he had seen Uncle Feldman in shul, Berka dug his fork viciously into his chicken but remained silent. Later that evening when Benjamin told her privately about his conversation with old Feldman, Berka suddenly seemed vulnerable to her. If you repeat a word of this conversation to Joel, she warned her brother, you will never set foot in this house again.

At eight o'clock she and Berka walked over to fetch Gittel. She was waiting at the gate in her blue dress. She protested all the way to the cinema that she should never have come. What would people say? Sheinka lying in hospital; no one to pour a glass of tea for Dovid, the child without a mother and Gittel Levitan goes to bioscope.

'They'll say it's about time that Gittel Levitan went to bioscope,' Berka said. 'Why didn't Raizel come, Yenta? She loves a good show. And there's a double feature tonight. Tom Mix in the 'Masked Riders' then Jeannette MacDonald and Nelson Eddy. If she's determined to be a nun okay, but at least she can go out with her parents.'

'She's got a headache, poor girl. Don't worry. Benjamin will be home early from Rabbi Josselson.'

'Some company, Benjamin,' he said leading his wife and sister-in-law into the cinema.

'So many chairs, such a high ceiling, just like in shul,' Gittel whispered, awed. 'It must be difficult to clear away the cobwebs. Look, there's Avram Stern and his family. They must be wondering what an old woman like me is doing in bioscope. And at such a time.'

'Sit here beside me, Gittel,' Berka said. 'I'll explain anything you don't understand.'

'So dark,' Gittel said, jumping nervously as the first clash of chords was heard. 'And such loud music. I can hardly hear the buzzing in my ears.'

'Those men are robbers,' Berka explained softly. 'They're riding towards the railway line where they plan to hold up the mail train and steal the money.'

Gittel began to cough as soon as the robbers appeared on their horses. They dismounted and hid behind some trees after laying sticks of dynamite on the rails.

'Someone should tell the train driver,' Gittel whispered to Berka. 'A person can get killed like that. Who knows? Maybe there are women and children on the train.'

At that moment the train appeared on the screen, moving rapidly towards the burning dynamite. Gittel sucked in her breath and grabbed Berka's arm. As the train roared towards the cameras, she cried out loudly and ducked.

It was with great difficulty that Berka persuaded her to remain in the cinema. She kept her eyes averted from the screen but cast sidelong glances at the fighting between Tom Mix's forces and the robbers. She coughed throughout the film.

At interval Berka took her into the foyer for a drink.

'Have you got a cold?' he asked.

'No, no. It's all that dust from the horses,' she said. 'It got into my throat.'

'Come Gittel, the dust has subsided,' he said. 'You'll like the main film better. No horses. It's a pity Raizel didn't come,' he said looking up Main Street. 'To tell the truth, Gittel, I'm a little worried about her. She looks so sad sometimes.'

'In my opinion, not that it counts, you should marry her off, Berka. Contact Yudaiken the matchmaker. For such a pretty girl you won't even need a large dowry. She doesn't meet the right people,' Gittel hesitated. 'And she's with married people too much. Miss Breen writes in the "Americaner" that . . .'

'Gittel, are you trying to tell me something?'

'Yes, no, of course not. Don't get cross, Berka. Raizel's a lovely girl but she needs a change, a holiday perhaps. Not that I believe in holidays but for some people it's good. Maybe it'll help her, maybe not. Absence, distance, is a great healer. Miss Breen . . .'

Berka had stopped listening. Gittel, he thought sadly, was becoming senile in that crazy household of hers.

'. . . and they lived happily ever after,' Dovid concluded, closing Grimm's fairy tales. 'Did you like that story?' he asked Ruth.

'I'm sorry for the ugly sisters. I like your stories and Zeide Berchik's stories best, even if they don't live happily ever after. Tattele, let's go to Schumacher's for an ice cream.'

It was a cool evening and the smell of Burger's honeysuckle filled the air. Such a big rough-looking man, Dovid thought as he and Ruth approached the Burgers' house. And such eyes. Their veranda was in darkness but a faint light shone through the frosted glass door. When Jan had stepped out of the bar the day before, his presence seemed to fill the street. Raizel should never have accepted his flowers. The girl was a flirt; she was encouraging his advances.

'Annatjie lives here,' Ruth whispered. 'She's also starting school on Monday. I said hello to her yesterday and she said hello back. From my hello she couldn't tell that I don't speak

English properly. Maybe she'll be my friend,' she added, trailing a finger lightly along the fence where the honeysuckle grew.

Raizel sat reading in the large cane chair, her feet tucked under her. A mere child and how harshly he judged her. She was simple, naive, and really believed that life was as uncomplicated as her novelettes. Man meets woman, they fall in love, have difficulties which are miraculously resolved and live happily ever after, like in fairy tales.

Ruth climbed onto the fence and called out: 'Raizel, my tatteh is going to buy me an ice-cream. Come, he'll buy you one too.'

Raizel looked up, startled. She glanced at Dovid who stood at the gate. He did not repeat the invitation.

'No thanks, Ruthie. I don't like ice-cream.'

'You don't like ice-cream?' Ruth echoed incredulously.

'Come along,' Dovid offered belatedly. 'If you like that is,' he added, glancing involuntarily towards Mrs. Pinn's house.

'If I dare to, you mean. And fall into Mrs. Pinn's black pit of a mouth.'

The mere child gave way to a mocking woman.

'No thanks, Ruthie. I don't like ice-cream.'

'Then stay,' he said angrily, as though she'd refused a gracious invitation. He pulled Ruth off the fence and walked away quickly.

With whom was he angry? Dovid put his trembling hands into his pockets. With Mrs. Pinn? With Raizel? Only with himself. He was afraid of the neighbours. No sooner had Sheinka gone into labour, they'd say, than Dovid began chasing after Raizel Feldman, using his daughter as a screen. Taking them for ice-cream. Indeed. Dovidke the hypocrite. He wanted to walk beside her in the dark of the summer's evening, enjoying her closeness . . .

Dovid caught his breath. His yearning began as an ache in the heart and spread all over his body, leaving him weak and breathless.

He loves her, Dovid Erlich the hypocrite. He loves her so much that as he walks up First Avenue saying good evening to this one and that one, accepting congratulations on the birth of his son, replying about the health of his wife, he can think of nothing but Raizel's soft white arms and the fresh scent of her hair. He wants to abandon his daughter to the dark streets of Mayfontein, as he solicitously enquires after Mrs. Hirshman's cats, and rush back to Raizel's veranda, kiss the contemptuous smile off her lips and crush her against him in view of a thousand Mrs. Pinns who might be lurking behind the lace curtains.

'I'm mad,' Dovid stopped to catch his breath as they approached Main Street. 'I'm a raving lunatic. From where do such thoughts come!'

'I'm tired, tatteh,' Ruth said following him breathlessly. 'You're walking too fast.'

Dovid bent down and kissed the top of her head, holding her against him as though to draw into himself her innocence and purity. Taking her by the hand he turned slowly into Main Street, breathing evenly in an effort to quieten his thumping heart.

But he could not throw off his feeling of rapture. He smiled happily at the people strolling in Main Street. Everyone was his friend.

'Ah,' he overheard Hershl say to Faigel after he had greeted them joyously, 'the birth of a son has made him happy at last.'

He bought the ice cream for Ruth, went through the motions of paying, talking and shaking hands with the Schumachers, then returned to First Avenue like a sleep-walker. As they approached Berka's house Ruth said she was thirsty.

'Get some water from Bobbe Yenta's kitchen,' he said letting her into the gate. He remained on the other side of the fence.

Raizel put down her book.

'I must speak to you,' he said quietly, urgently. 'I'm going to put Ruth to bed now. Come to the house in fifteen minutes.'

'What of Mrs. Pinn?' Raizel began but the mockery died on her lips. She dropped her eyes. 'I'll come,' she said softly and went into the house.

Exhausted by the rapid walk, Ruth fell asleep almost immediately. Dovid turned off the veranda light and sat in a corner, hidden from the street by the potted geraniums. The sound of the crushers pounded through his chest until he felt his heart would burst, and the scent of honeysuckle, mixed with that of the acrid geraniums, induced in him a state of light-headed ecstasy.'

70

When Raizel came onto the veranda he rose from his chair, feeling taller, stronger and more vital than he had ever felt in his life. He put his arm around her and led her into the darkened lounge.

His longings for Ragaza, his contempt for Africa, his rootlessness, anxieties and guilts melted in Raizel's arms. She clothed his discontented spirit with flesh and he was conscious of his body as he had never been with Vera or with Sheinka. For years he believed that he had abdicated from the emotional life, that all that remained was the search for the correct way of life. Now he moved beyond this. To hold Raizel in his arms was to hold life itself. More surely than if he had read it in the most respected, most hallowed book he learned, as he probed her sweetness, that if he ever let her go, he would lose life itself. And yet he saw, with almost frightening clarity, that this kind of happiness was not for him, that he was part of another design which would inexorably draw him away from life.

'Don't ever let me go,' Raizel cut across his forebodings. 'Nothing is as strong as my love for you. I feel in some way, Dovid, that if we lose one another, we are both lost.'

'I'm not real, Raizel. You're in love with a refugee from another existence.'

'I'm real, Dovid. Cling to me. I'm real enough for both of us. You say those things to frighten me, even if you half believe them yourself. Say rather that you've got real problems: Sheinka, the children. I won't be a burden Dovid. I won't make demands. We'll find a way and until then I'll wait. I just want to be part of your world.'

'Tomorrow,' he dismissed his hovering fears, 'tomorrow we'll talk sensibly. I've never felt like this before, Raizel. If there's anything, anyone, that could've recalled me from my past it would have been you. But Raizel, it's too late. My father should never have returned to Ragaza.'

When Gittel, Yenta and Berka walked onto the veranda they found Dovid sitting in a corner, gazing up at the stars. Gittel was ebullient. She even forgot her self-imposed reticence in Dovid's presence.

71

'Such a love story,' she told him. 'So tender, so pure. It was wonderful. I cried all the way through. He loves her and she loves him but she's married to an older man who is very good to her and in the end she gives up the lover. And they don't talk to each other like ordinary people, Dovid: they sing! Can you believe it! I didn't hear the buzzing in my ears right through the picture.'

'Once she got Tom Mix's dust out of her throat, she became a bioscope fan,' Berka said to Dovid who smiled indulgently at his mother-in-law, stripped of all resentment.

He'd never before felt so warmly towards Gittel. Love indeed created strange paradoxes.

8

*D*ovid felt the soft pressure of light on his eyelids. Through half-closed eyes he watched the autumn woodland scene stir to life as the sun filtered through the cotton curtains. On the curtains it was perennially autumn. The red and gold leaves fell to the ground under the oaks and the birches, and the tunnel-like paths stretched away to an infinity of red, brown and yellow. He took Raizel's hand and walked under the trees, feeling the crunch of dead leaves beneath his feet. I'm ten years older than you, he told her. You'll grow younger, I'll grow older, she replied. But in my soul, he said, it's perennially autumn.

For a long moment the whole world was golden and glowing, then the scene faded behind his closed eyes and he turned his face from the early morning light.

Gittel hummed a song from the film as she prepared the Sunday lunch. Ruth, who stood nearby rolling a piece of dough in imitation of her grandmother, looked up in surprise. She rarely heard Gittel sing. Everything was different when her mother was away. She never allowed Ruth to participate in the baking or the cooking. You're messing, she'd say crossly, wiping up the grains of flour from the kitchen floor.

'My first bris by a grandchild,' Gittel told Ruth. 'Chaim Leib has three sons in America but does he ever send me a photograph of them? It'll probably be my last bris as well,' she sighed. 'Your mother won't have any more children. Her pregnancy seemed like nine years not nine months. Poor Sheinkala. She doesn't know how to suffer. Anyway, we'll make a nice bris. There'll be plenty to eat and drink.'

'Didn't I have a bris?' Ruth asked.

'Oy vey, the questions she asks.'

When she had prepared the lunch, Gittel went into the backyard.

'Dora!' she called in the direction of the servant's room. 'Dora! Kum insite!'

A short black woman, dressed in one of Sheinka's discarded summer frocks, came running barefoot out of her room and stood at the kitchen door, waiting for instructions.

'Nu, kum shein insite, domkop!' Gittel said. 'Nem arop fun table, you chasershe shikshe, and vash die dishes.'

The girl looked at her, perplexed: Sheinka usually gave her instructions. In exasperation Gittel mimed the action of taking the dishes and cooking utensils off the table and washing them in the kitchen sink. The girl's face brightened with understanding.

'Stupid shikshe,' Gittel said to Dovid when he came into the kitchen. 'Doesn't understand a word of English. And she was born in this country.'

Dovid took his coffee and Sunday paper into the lounge. The room was permeated with Raizel's presence. He opened the paper but none of the words registered. Like a sleepwalker suddenly awakened to his nocturnal wanderings, he was reluctant to accept his aberrant behaviour. He had dreamed it; he had imagined it, as indeed he had many times before. He had not really held this yielding loving girl in his arms and poured into her ears the accumulated feelings of many years.

But as surely as he felt Sheinka's presence in the odour of Vicks which pervaded the house, so he was now aware of the perfume of Raizel's hair against the sofa on which he was sitting.

He stared up at the moulded iron ceiling, following the lines of intricate flowers and vines. How could he face Berka, Gittel, Sheinka, even Raizel? How could he expect this young vital girl to wait for him, in vain? Last night they had not spoken about the future. They had only decided that the English lessons were to stop.

If Sheinka was really as ill as she had always claimed . . .

Self-hatred brought on a rush of guilt feelings which he accepted with relief.

In the afternoon Dovid went to visit Sheinka. Ruth wandered about the house, lonely and listless. She stood on the veranda and watched the neighbourhood children walking towards the swimming bath which was at the edge of the plantation. The boys swaggered past with their towels around their necks, swinging their swimming trunks by the cord, and the girls carried neatly rolled towels under their arms. Moshe, Joshua and Daniel joined them, followed by the Burger children. Only Annatjie looked back at Ruth. She hesitated for a moment, then joined her brothers and sisters. Ruth had only been to the baths once last summer with Raizel, but had been too afraid to go into the water where the children splashed and threw one another around. With Annatjie, perhaps, it would have been different.

The adults were having their Sunday nap and the street was deserted except for Ruth and a few black servants who were sitting on the pavement in their Sunday clothes. From across the veld, beyond the plantation, came the sound of singing and drumming. The mine workers were having their Sunday dance. Ruth had seen them once, dressed in beads and feathers with rattles tied to their ankles. They stamped their feet wildly as they raised their assegais above their heads in a mock battle dance.

'It's only a dance,' Zeide Berchik had reassured Ruth when she shrank from the wild-looking men.

As the drumming started up, some of the servants rose from the pavement, dusted the red sand off their clothes and moved slowly towards the compound. Only Dora and her sister remained on the street corner.

'Sister, schmister,' Gittel said as she went into the kitchen to read her paper. 'They're all sisters and brothers. Like the beasts of the field they live. Their fathers they don't know but their sisters they know. No go avek,' she called out to Dora. 'Make fire in stoff in havanaver.' It had taken Dora months to find out that havanaver was thirty minutes.

Dora had an old black gramophone on the pavement on which she was playing a few scratched records over and over again. She and her sister stood near it, moving slowly to the repetitive rhythm. They began a slow mesmerising movement towards one another, retreated, came together again, whirling faster and faster in time to the music. Finally they sank onto the pavement, wiping the sweat from their faces.

'Too hot,' Dora's sister said reaching for a piece of sugar cane. She took it between her teeth, tore off the hard outer fibre and bit into the succulent centre, chewing it in time to the music. When she had sucked out the sweetness, she spat the pulp into the gutter.

'You want?' she offered Ruth who was watching her.

Ruth shook her head. She was afraid of black people. Her mother had told her stories about children in Lithuania who had been carried off by the gypsies. The schocherdikke, her mother warned, did the same.

'Shut up, you blerry kaffirs!' Mr. Burger shouted in Afrikaans from his veranda. 'A person can't sleep with all that blerry row going on. Voetsek! What do you think this is? A blerry location?'

They clucked agitatedly, picked up the gramophone and ran into the backyard. Ruth watched Mr. Burger pull at his braces in annoyance and shake a fist at the retreating servants. If she did become friendly with Annatjie, she decided, they would play in the veld.

Later in the afternoon, Gittel took Ruth with her to Yenta's house. In addition to the usual crowd of visitors who dropped in on a Sunday afternoon, Aaron Blecher and his wife were expected for tea. Today they were the guests of honour. Aaron had recently bought a Nash and he was coming all the way from Greenside to show them the car. He was the first of the landsleit to own one.

Zutzke and the other neighbourhood dogs barked wildly as the large black car came down First Avenue, hooting at non-existent obstacles. Aaron was a small man and one could barely see his head above the steering wheel.

'A real circus,' Berka muttered. If Aaron hadn't played such a good game of bloff and if Berka hadn't known him for so many years, he would have cut relations with him. Yet in spite of that orange-brick house in Greenside and this hearse-like car, Aaron was a good man. The outer trappings of wealth, Berka decided as he watched Mrs. Blecher wipe the dust off the bonnet with a yellow duster, were his wife's doing.

After a lavish tea, the women gathered on the veranda and

the men went into the dining-room for their game of poker.

'We've got a minyan,' Berka told Benjamin who was hovering about expectantly as the players took their seats. 'Holy men shouldn't gamble, especially if they haven't got with what.'

Benjamin shrugged and walked around the table slowly, saying grace after tea.

'Baruch ata Adonai . . . throw out the queen,' he whispered to Leib Schwartzman in passing, 'eloheinu melech . . .'

'Perhaps you've got a prayer for four aces?' Leib asked him.

'Ahah! A gambler's den, a poker school,' Sam the barber said, walking into the room.

'School!' Aaron said scornfully, shuffling the cards. 'What school? A kindergarten. Come join us. Show these kailikes how it's done in the higher institutions of learning.'

'What's your limit? I may not be able to afford it.'

'Four bob.'

'Too high,' Sam laughed standing behind Berka. 'So, Berrala, playing bloff. Der rebbe meg, eh? Don't in future, throw me one of your pained looks as you pass by my barbershop with honest beads of sweat on your brow. Greyhound racing is as honourable as poker.'

'Tell me, Sam, what are the ethics of your poker school?' Leib asked. 'You know, some declare penalties, others don't. How's it by you?'

'No ethics, no limit,' Sam replied moving over behind Aaron. 'Poker isn't a game; it's a way of life. And all's fair in the rotten game of life. Like in love.'

Dovid came into the room and was greeted warmly by all the players.

'Dovidke!' Raizel heard the chorus of voices from the kitchen. 'Mazeltov, mazeltov! Have lots of nachas from your son. How's Sheinka?'

Raizel clattered the cups in the sink in an effort to drown their voices. Only the birth of a son was important enough to interrupt a game of poker. She gave Ruth a dishcloth to dry the dishes.

'That's a good husband. Instead of playing bloff on a Sunday afternoon, he goes off to visit his wife. What? He doesn't gamble? Ever? Dovidke, what you need is a few interesting vices. You're going to be very lonely in Heaven without your friends. You should sin occasionally . . .'

Raizel did not hear Dovid's reply. Play was resumed. 'Double . . . ahaha, he's got a pair of twos already so he doubles . . . I'll see you . . . So, a bloff, eh? A Yiddishe forest he's got, tree trees . . .'

'Hello,' Dovid said at the kitchen door. Ruth dropped the dishcloth and ran up to him.

'Can he speak yet?' she asked.

'You'll teach him when he comes home, my love. Hello Raizel.'

She looked at him and smiled wanly.

'Hello Dovid. How's everyone?'

'All right. Sheinka's reconciled to the loss of her Vicks. In an emergency they can give her oxygen. The baby looks less red and crumpled than he did yesterday. How are you?'

'Fine.' She took a side of pickled beef out of the ice box and began to slice it. 'But it's going to be harder than I thought. Ruthie, please take these plates into the dining room for me.'

Ruth looked at them both, then walked slowly out of the kitchen with the plates.

'What is it?' Dovid asked.

'Guilts, anger, jealousy. I didn't count on that.'

'I'm sorry.'

'Don't be. I'm not.'

'You'll stay for supper, Dovid,' Yenta said coming into the kitchen. 'And do me a favour. Run across and call in Hershl and Faigel. They should bring the children also. I've got enough to feed the whole of First Avenue.'

'It's the last hand, it's the last hand,' the players protested when Yenta eventually placed the large plate of meat in the centre of the table. 'Yentala, have mercy. I've got my losses to make up. I'm three shillings down. The last hand, we promise. Deal, Jankala, deal.'

Aaron sighed contentedly when supper was over, and sipping his lemon tea loudly said:

'It's good to be back in Mayfontein again, among friends. In Greenside everyone has a quarter acre with his house facing north and you don't see a soul. Here there's still a feeling of landsmanschaft. Everyone on his veranda each concerned for the other . . .'

'Especially Mrs. Pinn,' Berka growled.

'It's strange you should say so, Aaron,' Hershl said. 'Only on Friday I was lamenting the lack of community feeling. But I suppose we've little to complain of.'

'It won't last,' Aaron shook his head sadly. 'Already the old landsmanschaft is disintegrating. At the Workers' Club which used to be my second home, I'm becoming an outcast, an anomaly. After all, I'm an employer of labour, an exploiter. As one becomes richer one becomes lonelier, I'm telling you. Before we travelled in trams like everyone else; today we travel alone, in a hearse as Berka calls it.'

'It should happen to me,' Leib said wistfully looking at the Nash around which the neighbourhood children had gathered. 'I undertake to travel in a hearse like yours, Aaron, for as long as I live.'

'You can have it,' Berka said knocking out his pipe against his shoe. 'I'm not for the new way of living. In Mayfontein we eat in the house and shit in the yard, like normal human beings. In Greenside they eat in the garden and shit in the house. The rich acquire very dirty habits.'

'The ladies, the ladies!' Hershl protested.

'What's the matter, Reb Hershl, don't ladies defecate?'

'Vey, vey, such vulgarity,' Yenta said rising from her chair. 'Come, ladies. Let's go inside and leave the men to their elevated talk.'

Dovid sat for a while listening to the usual arguments and discussions. He was bored. How could he have participated in it all these years?

'No English tonight?' Berka asked him. 'It's quiet in the kitchen. No one will disturb you.'

'I've graduated,' Dovid said quietly. 'It's just practice that I need now. Besides, Ruthie starts school tomorrow and I want to put her to bed early. It's going to be a long hard day for her.'

Dovid went past the lounge where the women were sitting, into the kitchen where Raizel was washing the dishes.

'Raizel,' he said in a trembling voice that brought an apprehensive look into her eyes. 'I want you to know that whatever happens I'll never stop loving you.'

He turned away and walked quickly out of the kitchen, leaving her to stare after him in dismay.

9

*I*t had rained during the night and the tall veld grass was wet and shiny in the early morning sun.

'Mind the puddle!' Raizel called out to Ruth who dawdled along behind her on the school path.

As Ruth jumped over the puddle the crayons and sandwiches gave a hollow thump in the otherwise empty school case. Discouraged by Raizel's brief impatient replies, Ruth had fallen some distance behind her and worried in silence about the difficulties that lay ahead. When must she eat her sandwiches? Was there a lavatory at school? Would her teacher be cross because she couldn't speak English properly? So far Raizel's advice had been far from reassuring.

'If the children call you Bolshie, take no notice. If they call you bloody Jew, tell the teacher.'

Ruth vowed that if they called her anything at all she would run away. She would creep quietly into the house, release Zutzke who had been locked up that morning, take food from the ice box and go and live in the plantation forever.

'It doesn't matter if she's early,' Raizel told Dovid when she called for Ruth. 'She's registered. All she has to do is to go into classroom number two when the bell rings. I can't wait, I have to be at work by eight.'

Ruth had seen the school many times from the outside. It was a low, L-shaped red brick building with sash windows which stood at the southern-most part of the suburb near the houses of the mine officials. She had passed close by one morning with Gittel. The children sat in pairs at wooden desks and chanted in unison:

'A is for Apple, B is for . . .'

She forgot what B was for but at least she knew one lesson, Ruth thought as she brushed the glittering raindrops off the grass.

Raizel opened the creaking iron gate and walked into the grounds of the school. There was not a soul in sight. Ruth sighed with relief at the unexpected reprieve.

'There isn't school today?' she asked hopefully.

'Of course there is. It's still early and no one's here yet. Come Ruth. Classroom number two is at the other end. Sit on this step and soon the other children will arrive. There's nothing to be afraid of,' she said impatiently as the tears welled up in Ruth's eyes. 'Everyone will be here soon. I can't wait. Don't be afraid,' she added gently, giving Ruth her handkerchief. 'I asked Hershl's boys to look after you.'

Ruth sat down on the step with her case in her lap, restraining an impulse to run after Raizel as she disappeared down the corridor. She felt utterly desolate. Only the roar of the crushers, the crickets in the veld and the chirping of the sparrows in the wet grass provided continuity with her previous existence. Through the double row of bluegums which grew outside the school fence, she could see the veld and the long straight rows of houses at its edge. The dusty roads, the people, the dumps, all seemed dear to her, though lost forever. Bobbe Gittel was in the kitchen now, shouting at Dora; Zutzke was locked up in the bathroom, whining and scratching at the door. Her eyes filled with tears again. Perhaps she should return, tell Bobbe Gittel that school was only starting tomorrow . . .

It was no good. They'd only shout and bring her back to school; the teacher would be angry and the children would laugh. She dried her eyes with Raizel's handkerchief and looked at her new surroundings. A square of asphalt led off from the school building and all around it was a dusty play area which had been levelled and cleared of grass. A black-spiked iron fence surrounded the school.

Several games of hopscotch were drawn on the asphalt. Did they teach hopscotch at school, she wondered? She had never been asked to play with the neighbourhood children but had watched them so often that she knew the game. She would practise before anyone arrived. Perhaps when they saw how well she played, they would not laugh at her English.

Near the fence she found a flat stone. Holding her case in one hand, she threw the goon into square one, then hopped on one foot, driving it forward from one compartment to another, careful to clear the lines. When she had successfully completed the first round, she bent down to pick up her goon.

'She's got blue broekies!' She heard laughter at the gate, 'Kom kyk maar! I saw her broekies when she picked up the goon!'

'Baby's got blue broekies! Yirreh! She's gonna cry. Ag man, she's just a big cry baby with blue broekies!' The tallest of the four boys smirked as he passed by.

She did not raise her eyes from the ground.

'Baby's got blue broekies!' His lieutenant echoed, coming towards her.

'Go avay,' she said, large-eyed with fear. 'I'll call a poleesman to chop arop your head.'

The boys began to laugh, clutching at their stomachs with exaggerated gestures of uncontrollable mirth.

'A Bolshie, a Bolshie!' they called to one another. 'A Bolshie with blue broekies!'

Ruth felt the tears prickling her nose and she turned away her face.

'Leave her alone,' she heard a familiar voice. She turned around and saw Moshe, Joshua and Daniel approaching. Moshe was taller and sturdier than the largest of the blond boys.

'Ag, you ous can't take a joke. Man, we was only playing, we wasn't doing nothing. We was just laughing because she can't speak English,' he said, walking away.

'If they start with you again, tell me,' Moshe said casually. 'And if they tease you about broeks and things, just say "clean, washed and paid for".'

'Clean, washed and paid for,' Ruth repeated softly to herself as she watched Daniel walk away between his two big brothers. Of what use was a baby brother in the nursing home? Nobody would tease Daniel today.

The playground began to fill rapidly. From a distance she saw Annatjie with her older sister. When Annatjie made a movement towards Ruth, her sister jerked her back roughly.

'You can't play with them,' she said loudly. 'They killed Jesus Christ.'

Ruth remained on the step while the children milled around, ignoring her. When the bell rang, they all hurried off towards the classrooms. She followed Daniel into classroom number two. There was a rush for desks and when everyone was seated, Ruth still stood near the platform, clutching her case.

'There's place here,' a dark-haired girl called out from the back.

Ruth went over quickly and sat down.

'My name's Mavis. My father's a foreman on the mine and I've got a big sister in Standard Five. What's your name?'

'Ruth,' she replied.

She did not know the English word for her father's trade and a baby brother in a nursing home seemed a poor offering compared to a sister in Standard Five.

A tall gaunt woman with glasses and short hair came into the classroom.

'Good morning, children,' she said in a booming voice. 'You must all stand up when I come into the classroom and say "Good morning, Miss MacCarthy".'

Amid shuffling of desks, cases and feet they stood up and repeated:

'Good morning, Miss MacCarthy.'

'Now leave your cases at your desks. All the Jewish children come over to this side and the Christian children go to the other side.'

A pogrom! Ruth panicked. She looked across the classroom at Daniel. When she saw no sign of fear from him, she calmed down and moved away from her desk with the other Jewish children.

'Every morning before lessons, we have Bible classes,' came the belated explanation. 'The Jewish children will remain here for Old Testament with Miss Greenblatt and the Christian children will move into classroom three for New Testament with me. Onwards Christian soldiers! Single file! Quick march!'

The Jewish children from classroom three filed into the room, accompanied by Miss Greenblatt, a mild-mannered woman who crossed her legs carefully as she sat down behind the table. She began to tell them the story of Adam and Eve. Ruth listened intently; she had never heard it before. The description of Eden sounded like der heim; the world into which Adam and Eve were exiled, like the veld in winter. She shuddered at Miss Greenblatt's description of the serpent: long, black, slimy, with an evil smile and a soft voice. All that trouble, just for eating an apple.

'Any questions, children?' Miss Greenblatt asked.

For a while there was silence. Then Daniel put up his hand. He blushed as he stood up.

'If Adam and Eve were the first people in the world,' he asked hesitantly, 'who did their children marry?'

'If I didn't know your father, Daniel, I would think you were being cheeky,' Miss Greenblatt said, looking flustered. 'Don't ask such silly questions in future. It is written like that in the Bible and we don't question the Bible.'

Daniel looked thoroughly miserable as he sat down. He did not look up again until the Bible class was over.

'Every morning,' Miss MacCarthy said when she returned to the classroom, 'I will take the register. When I call out your name you must answer "Present please", and I will put a tick next to your name.'

'Present please,' Ruth practised silently with each child.

'Anna Burger,' Miss MacCarthy called, glancing up at each child in turn. Anna sat in the front row. Ruth looked sadly at her straggly blond plaits. They would never be friends now. Her sister thought that Ruth had killed Jesus Christ.

'Present please,' Ruth answered correctly when her name was called.

The time passed quickly. With a wooden stick Miss MacCarthy pointed to a drawing of a large red apple and said:

'Repeat after me: A is for apple . . .'

She went from the yellow banana to the black cat, to the brown spotted dog, to the white egg, then returned to the apple.

'The apple,' she said with a smile, 'is the beginning of all knowledge. Now repeat after me: A is for . . .'

When the bell rang for the play break, the children began to rummage in their cases for sandwiches. Ruth drew out her brown paper bag and followed Mavis outside.

'Let's sit at the fence, under the trees,' Mavis said unwrapping a neat packet of sandwiches. Ruth opened her paper bag and took out a thick bread and butter sandwich that had come unstuck. She pressed it together and opening her mouth wide, took a bite. Mavis drew out a thinly-sliced sandwich, covered with bits of lettuce.

'What a funny sandwich,' she said watching Ruth take another bite. 'So thick! That's the way my mother cuts bread for our native servant.'

Ruth flushed and while Mavis dusted off a large rock next to the fence, Ruth returned the sandwich to the paper bag. She sat down on the rock next to Mavis.

'Aren't you eating any more?' Mavis asked.

'I not hungaray,' Ruth flushed. Her pronunciation had betrayed her at last.

'You speak funny,' Mavis said.

At the expected rejection, Ruth got up and started to walk away.

'Hey, don't go!' Mavis called out. 'I'm sorry. It doesn't matter how you speak. You can be my friend.'

Ruth looked at her gratefully and returned to the rock.

'Shame, look at that stray dog at the dustbin,' Mavis said in dismay. 'He's starving. His ribs stick out. Poor thing.'

Ruth got up and walked over to the dog. He snarled as she approached him. Remaining at a safe distance, she threw him a piece of her bread and butter. He moved hesitantly towards it, his streaming eyes blinking suspiciously. He snapped it up, then stood still, waiting for more. By the time she had fed him all her sandwiches, he allowed Ruth to pat him. Mavis stood behind her, watching with approval.

Suddenly Ruth saw a foot shoot out in front of her. It landed with a dull thud against the dog's ribs. He gave a loud yelp of pain and with his tail between his legs, dashed out of the school grounds, whining all the while. Ruth looked up and saw Paul Stern standing over her, smiling.

'Serves him right, the dirty dog. You're just a stupid Gingy to feed him. He'll die all the same. Cry baby!' he said as Ruth's pent-up emotions burst through. With his shirt tails flying, he ran away to join the boys in a game of bok-bok.

'You . . . snake!' she screamed after him, crying uncontrollably. 'I hate you! I hate you!'

Mavis put her arm around Ruth's shoulders and led her back to their rock.

'Do you know him?' she asked, shaken but dry-eyed.

'Yes, his fader is Avremala der hinner Yid. Sells chickens,' she explained. It was a long story. When she could speak English she would tell Mavis how Paul always travelled on the cart with his father, holding the reins of the horses, whipping them to go faster and shouting 'Whoooooaaa!' when he wanted them to stop. Although he was only a year or two older than Ruth, she always thought of him as a big boy, especially when he was perched high up on his father's chicken cart. 'Gingy!' he would mouth when she stood next to the cart while Bobbe Gittel chose a squawking chicken from the netted cages. A wild boy, Gittel would console Ruth. His father should give him a taste of the whip. Poor horses.

In Mavis's company, Ruth gradually regained her composure and put the unfortunate dog out of her mind. Until the end of break they sat in the shade, breathing in the smell of damp grass, bluegums and bread and butter. She had a friend. It didn't matter that Annatjie wasn't allowed to play with her; Mavis Jackson was her friend. She didn't care if others laughed at her English; Mavis understood her.

When she returned to the classroom it was almost like coming home. The drawings of the apple, the banana, the cat and the dog looked down benignly at her. The children looked more familiar, Miss MacCarthy less frightening. She was glad to be at school.

'I live in that house, the one with the mosquito netting,' Mavis said when they parted at the gate. 'Rand Mines isn't far, just over the veld. Will your mother let you come and play? Do you like chips? The ones from Davis?'

'Yes,' Ruth lied. She had never tasted them. Sheinka said they were fried in dirty oil.

'Then bring a sixpence tomorrow and we'll go up to Main Street after school to buy some. Goodbye.'

Ruth joined the long row of children who were walking over the veld towards Mayfontein. Annatjie's brothers, Dirk and Uys ran ahead, tying trip knots in the long supple grass. They were followed by Moshe and Joshua who pretended not to see the knots and ran through them, falling over into the damp grass. Then they ran ahead, tying knots for Dirk and Uys to trip over. Daniel walked along the path with the smaller boys and girls. Trip knots was a game for big boys. The game would end at the edge of the veld when Moshe and his brothers and the Burger boys would part. Mr. Burger had forbidden them to play with Jewish children.

Ruth remained at the tail end of the row. As she jumped over the puddle which had almost dried up since that morning, she heard the hollow thud of crayons in her case. Tomorrow she would leave them at home. Miss MacCarthy had promised them pastels and coloured clay if they remembered their lesson.

'A is for Epple,' she practised as she walked along.

How small the houses looked, how distant the suburb was. Even the mine dumps had shrunk since that morning. She looked back at the school, then again at the dumps: They had lost their splendour, their air of sanctuary.

Jones the iceman stood outside Leib Schwartzman's house and all the children rushed across the street towards his cart, catching the chips of ice as he sawed a portion off the main block for Chaya. Ruth loved the taste of sacking and sand in Jones's ice but she did not run up to the cart as usual. Gittel and Zutzke were waiting for her at the gate. Zutzke sped joyously towards her, licking her hands and face as she bent down to embrace him. She waited with Gittel for the postman, who brought only accounts. Ruth put her arms around her grandmother's hips and said softly:

'Maybe it'll come tomorrow. When I'm big and I go away from home, I'll write to you very often.'

'Such consolation she gives me,' Gittel smiled. 'Come. Lunchtime.'

Gittel took out the remains of the sabbath chicken from the ice chest. As she cut it into portions she sang softly:

> A brivale die mamen,
> Zolst du mein kind nisht varzamen . . .

She always sang that song when the postman had no letters for her.

'Oy vey,' she sighed, bringing the chicken to the table. 'Which part do you prefer, child?'

Ruth flushed with pleasure; she'd never been asked before.

'The wing,' she said casually.

'Funny,' Gittel said. 'You always eat the drumstick. Tell me, how was school?'

'Nice. And I've got a friend. Mavis Jackson.'

'Jackson. Is she Jewish?'

'No. She's asked me to come and play with her after school tomorrow. She's going to teach me to speak English properly,' Ruth added with newly-found guile.

'Good, good. But don't eat in their house. It's not kosher. I'll give you extra semitches with schmaltz tomorrow. Say you're not hungry if they offer you food. God forbid, they can noch give you pork to eat. Ugggh.'

'Bobbe,' Ruth said hesitantly. 'Can you make my semitches a little thinner tomorrow? The children laugh at me and say only kaffirs eat such thick slices of bread. Please make them thin.'

'New fashions,' Gittel sniffed. 'If it's thin you might as well eat paper. All right, all right, don't cry. Straight away there are tears. I don't know who you take after. I'll cut them thinner. New fashions,' she grumbled walking into the backyard. 'These kaffertes have to be watched,' she told Ruth. 'In no time at all they can stuff some washing into their bosoms and you wouldn't even know the difference.'

After lunch Ruth sat on the back steps and watched the large white sheets and towels flapping in the afternoon breeze. Mondays smell of fried fish and soap and wet clothes, she noted. And tomorrow will smell of chips and vinegar. On the way back from Davis's she would show Mavis her secret place in the plantation where she and Zutzke hid away during pogroms.

But perhaps Mavis didn't understand about pogroms. Besides, Berka said there would never be pogroms again. A heavy load lifted from her heart at the thought.

'Peachies! Peachies!' she heard a call from the street.

'Bobbe, they're selling peachies,' she called.

'Ask the wagoner to wait,' Gittel said taking a final count of the washing on the line. 'And in my chestadraw where I keep my underwear you'll find my purse. Please fetch it for me.'

Ruth went inside, darted around the breakfast room table and opened the top drawer of the chest of drawers. Under a cotton petticoat she found the little black purse. She was almost out of the room when she stopped, shook the purse, then opened it cautiously. There were two half crowns, a shilling and a sixpence. With a beating heart she took the shilling out of the purse. She held it in her palm for a few seconds, then hurriedly put it back again, running outside where Gittel stood on the pavement next to a large covered ox wagon.

'How much?' Gittel asked the sunburned man as he stepped off the wagon.

'Two shillings a bucket, a big bucket,' he answered in a thick voice. 'Three and six for two buckets, big buckets.'

'Three shillings,' Gittel bargained, walking towards the back of the wagon, followed by Ruth.

A smell of dry grass, dung and peaches rose from the dark interior of the wagon. The nearest half of the wagon was filled with small yellow peaches. Behind the peaches sat a thin woman in a dirty cotton dress, feeding a baby. Ruth watched with curiosity as the mother held her long sagging breast to the infant's mouth. There were three other children in the wagon, the biggest of whom climbed over the peaches and jumped off. He wore a pair of khaki shorts and a torn shirt which had once been white. His feet were caked with dirt and he had a running sore on his knee.

'Got some bread?' he asked Ruth quietly.

She nodded and went into the house. On the kitchen table stood half a white loaf. She walked out with the bread behind her back. Gittel might shout, though she herself gave bread to the black piccanins who came to the door.

'Give him, give him,' Gittel said as Ruth approached the wagon slowly. 'Business is business and I'm not paying more than three shillings for the peaches. But the family must eat. Bring out the brown loaf also. I'll get fresh bread from Hershl later on.'

The boy tore off a piece of bread and climbed onto the wagon again. He was waiting for Ruth at the gate when she came out with the other loaf.

The father did not appear to have seen anything. He carried the peaches into the house for Gittel, climbed onto the wagon and the boy led away the oxen.

'It's very hard,' Ruth told Dovid when he came home that evening. 'Some things I don't understand. Like A is for eppel. B is for benana, that's all right. But C is for cat? C is for semitches or, or,' she searched the kitchen for a suitable word, 'C is for saucer. I don't understand.'

'Don't worry. Just listen and you'll understand in time. I also say A is for eppel. But one day you'll say it correctly. For me it's too late to learn.'

After supper Raizel and Berka came to the house. Berka gave Ruth a beery kiss.

'Is Bobbe Yenta cross with you?' she asked crinkling up her nose.

'No,' he laughed, 'I didn't kiss her so she didn't smell the beer on my breath. Everything she knows, this child. So, how was school?'

She told them about the lessons, about her new friend and about Miss Greenblatt's anger with Daniel. She omitted only the incidents of the blue broekies and of Paul Stern kicking the dog.

'It is written,' Berka said angrily when he heard Daniel's question about Adam and Eve. 'Holy. It is written. Don't question the Bible. The first thing they learn in school is don't question. Tell me, Ruthie, what do you most want to learn at school?'

'Words,' she said gravely. 'I want to know the names of everything. Miss Greenblatt said that Adam gave names to all the cattle and all the fowls and all the beasts. I want to know them all.'

'You will,' Berka assured her. 'I've never known a woman who was at a loss for words. Don't tell Miss Greenblatt I said so but personally I think it was Eve, not Adam, who gave everything names. And I'm sure she had names for Adam himself that they wouldn't dare print in the Bible.'

When Dovid tucked Ruth into bed later that evening she asked:

'Tatteh, how do you say schnaider in English? I want to tell Mavis tomorrow what you do. Her father is a foreman on the mines.'

'Tailor,' he told her. 'And now sleep my child. You've had a busy day.'

For a while she lay in the dark repeating her lessons softly to Zutzke. 'A is for eppel . . . serpent . . . tree of . . .' She forgot what kind of tree it was but it did have apples on it. 'Present please . . . hungry, hun-gry . . . clean, washed and paid for . . .'

Then she sat up. Tomorrow after school she was going to buy chips with Mavis. She crept quietly out of bed and tip-toed to the chest of drawers. She opened it carefully, took out the black purse and felt in the dark the half crown and the shilling. She took out the shilling, tied it into her handkerchief as she had seen Yenta do, then put it under her pillow.

If she fell asleep quickly, tomorrow would come sooner.

10

'She'll be a different child now that she's at school,' Berka said when Dovid returned to the veranda. 'She's been with adults too much and has soaked up all their troubles. The child understands more than we think.'

'Indeed she does,' Dovid said sitting down on a chair opposite Raizel. If he stretched out his hand he could smoothe out the frown from her forehead. 'Has Benjamin left yet?'

'He leaves tomorrow, may he go in good health,' Berka said. 'What did the doctor say about him, Gittel?' He turned to his sister-in-law who was standing in the doorway.

'Poor Benjamin. The veins around his heart are calcified. He must lose weight and he must get stronger glasses, he's half blind. All alone in that dorp with no one to look after him. That's a life?'

'I've got a match for him,' Berka said drily. 'A woman with several daughters whom he can treat like his own. If he hadn't gone to the doctor I'd never have believed that he had a heart, even a calcified one.'

'Berka!' Gittel said reproachfully.

'Come for a stroll to our house, Gittel. Let's see how Yenta's bottling is getting on. I hear you also bought peaches today. Are you coming home, Raizel?'

'Later, Dad. I want a book from Dovid.'

Gittel looked from Dovid to Raizel, then sat down on the chair Berka had vacated.

'I won't come, Berka,' she said opening her newspaper. 'I'm tired. Today was washing day and the girl had to be watched all the time. I must also finish reading the "Americaner" by tomorrow. That's when I pass it onto Chaya.'

'No is no,' Berka shrugged. 'There were times when the ladies liked to walk with me. I must go and rescue Joel from that bore Benjamin. Since supper he's been closeted up in his room with the holy man. Poor boy, he must be crazy with boredom already.'

'Have you got another book for me?' Raizel asked Dovid sulkily.

She was frustrated by Gittel's stolid presence and angered by Dovid's helplessness. This was not how she imagined love. She wanted to be pursued, swept off her feet and borne away by a masterful man who would deal adequately with a suspicious mother-in-law. Dovid simply sat there looking at her with big soulful eyes, as Ruth had done that morning, doing nothing, saying nothing, accepting his fate. More than that: shaping his fate. He would never leave Sheinka; they would never become lovers; she would never be a part of his life.

'Try this one,' Dovid said. 'I took it out of the library last week but the humour's beyond me. Dickens's serious novels I understand but 'Piekviek Papers' is beyond me. I don't understand English humour.'

You don't understand any humour, Raizel wanted to scream. You don't know how to laugh at all, especially at yourself. "Piekviek Papers." Why did I ever imagine myself in love with you?

As she took the book his slender hands enclosed hers. She flushed deeply and turning to Gittel said:

'Good night, tante Gittel.'

'Good night, my child,' Gittel smiled benignly. She had become so engrossed in the latest instalment of 'The Dark Stranger' that she had forgotten her vigil. Nothing moved her as much as a sad love story.

Dovid went into the lounge and pressed his head against the sofa. The smell of Raizel's hair had all but gone. He must end this madness. Raizel was both kinswoman and strange fruit. If 'Pickwick Papers' was alien to him, how much more so was she? She had something of the pagan in her and her strong but mistaken passions recognised no boundaries. And what was love without compassion or obligation? More was involved than the practical difficulties of leaving a wife and children. She did not understand that the very act of deserting Sheinka would poison their relationship. Could one build a life on a despicable act, he had asked her. Can one build a life on a lie, she countered.

Poor misguided child. Love in her eyes condoned everything. I'll be your mistress, she offered, speaking like a character from a romantic novel. Dovid smiled at the sheer absurdity of the idea. In books, at least, lovers were conveniently provided with private incomes and with a place where they could meet. He could not even exchange a few words with Raizel without his mother-in-law breathing down his neck. Should he perhaps take a monthly loan from Steinberg the butcher and rent an apartment?

They belonged to different, irreconcilable worlds. He could not even say to her 'I love you'; it sounded false to his ears. 'Ich lieb dir' would fall strangely on hers. When he spoke Yiddish to her she often looked puzzled, as though he were a stranger. When he spoke English, he felt bereft of dignity as he slurred his 'r's', mispronounced the 'a', and hesitated over the 'th'.

But beyond the verbal barrier lay a deeper problem. He was not even sure that love meant the same thing to them. His doubts were reinforced when he listened to her records. 'I can't give you anything but love, ba-by!'

What had this to do with the way he felt about Raizel; the anguish, the desire, the hopelessness of it all?

'Tatteh! Tatteh!' Ruth called out, 'Please come. I'm having bad dreams again.'

Dovid sat on the bed with her and stroked her damp brow.

'It was horrible,' she said drawing close to him. 'A big black snake came out of the peaches in the wagon and bit the baby, and although I was watching I knew that the baby was me. Don't go away. Sing me a song and stay till I fall asleep. I'm afraid of that black snake.'

He lay down beside her and sang softly.

> Wie ken ich in finstern wald,
> Fargessen die liebe zu dir?
> Dermon ich mir dain gestalt,
> Ervekt zich a weitik in mir . . .

94

How can I in this dark wood,
Forget my love for you,
Your image haunts my memory
And re-awakens the pain in my heart.

When Ruth woke the next morning she slipped her hand under the pillow: the money was still there. She dressed quickly, slipped the knotted-up money into her bloomers and went into the kitchen where Gittel was reluctantly cutting thin sandwiches for her.

'New fashions,' she said wrapping the sandwiches in a piece of brown paper.

Ruth walked slowly along the school path. It was still early but the sun was already hot. She stopped at a bush of four o'clocks and plucked the half-open flowers off the stems, threading them onto a long piece of grass. This necklace will be for Mavis, she decided as she tied the succulent end of the grass to its flowering head. With her case in one hand and the necklace in the other, she walked slowly through the veld, humming softly to herself. As she approached the school she felt a momentary stab of anxiety, but when she remembered that after school she was going to buy chips with Mavis, she walked on resolutely. She looked down at her necklace of four o'clocks. Perhaps Mavis would think it a silly present. She hesitated, then threw it into the grass.

'Are you coming to me after school?' Mavis asked as they walked into the classroom.

'Yes,' Ruth replied. 'I got money from Bobbe Gittel. For chips.'

In spite of her impatience for their adventure to begin, school passed quickly and pleasantly. In Bible class they heard the story of Noah and his Ark. Daniel sat silently through the lesson and when Miss Greenblatt invited questions, he looked out of the window.

After they had repeated their lesson to Miss MacCarthy's satisfaction, she handed them small squares of rough black paper and a few pastels. She walked up and down the aisles, stopping every now and again to look at a drawing. Ruth was completely absorbed in her work. She drew two yellow mine dumps in one corner and a yellow sun with rays shining out of a horizontal strip of blue sky. Next to the mine dumps she drew two green trees with bunches of red cherries in them.

'Very good,' Miss MacCarthy said. 'Very good indeed, Ruth.'

She held it up for everyone to see, turning it this way and that. Ruth dropped her head; her heart was bursting with joy.

'You can take it home to show your mother,' Miss MacCarthy said, 'and tomorrow we'll pin it onto the wall.'

At playtime she and Mavis sat down on the rock under the trees. From a distance she saw Paul playing football with the other boys. Once, when the ball rolled near them he retrieved it and called out, 'Hello Gingey. How's the dog?' Ruth looked away angrily. The poor stray was nowhere to be seen.

'Bully!' Mavis said softly when he was out of earshot.

Ruth felt loved and protected.

'Your sandwiches smell nice,' Mavis said. 'I'll change one with you.'

Ruth gave Mavis the thinnest of her schmaltz sandwiches but remembering Gittel's warning, refused to accept one in return.

'I'm not hun-gry,' she said, pleased with her pronunciation.

'I'm not hungry,' Mavis corrected.

Ruth was puzzled. Then why did she take the schmaltz sandwich?

After school they walked to Mavis's house. It was a small corrugated iron cottage which was surrounded by a well-kept garden. The interior was dark and hot, in spite of the open windows.

'Ma's gone to the shops,' Mavis's sister told her. She was a tall blond girl with a thick plait hanging down her back. 'You're to take the fried fish from the ice chest and have a glass of milk. There's only one piece left so you'll have to share.'

'I don't want lunch. We're going to buy chips at Davis's. And you can't come with us,' Mavis taunted. 'Ruth's got money.'

'She never shares with me,' Mavis said as they walked over the veld towards Main Street.

Ruth was overjoyed. This was even better than having your own sister.

She waited outside the shop while Mavis bought the chips. Faint misgivings stirred in her as she watched Ron Davis fry the chips. Perhaps the oil was dirty; perhaps it wasn't kosher.

But when Mavis came out of the shop with the newspaper packet, the smell of chips smothered in vinegar and salt dispelled all her qualms. They did not open the packet until they reached the narrow backstreet to the north of Main Street which ran parallel to the railway line. Each took a turn in holding the chips and they ate slowly, savouring each one. As Ruth pressed the chips against her palate with her tongue, she thought that she had never eaten anything as delicious before. While she ate she talked rapidly and at great length. If Mavis did not always follow her, she gave no sign of it.

When they had worked down to the bottom of the packet, Mavis licked her fingers, crumbled the paper into a ball and threw it over the fence onto the railway line. They watched until a train passed over it, then returned over the veld to Mavis's house, playing trip knots all along the way.

With her drawing in her case and with a lightness of heart such as she had never felt before, Ruth returned home. Her only regret was that she had not saved a chip for Zutzke who sniffed at her hands.

'Take your tings and voetsek from here!' she heard Gittel shout in the backyard. 'Choleria, genavte! A kraink zol dir avekleigen!'

'I didn't take it missis. 'Strues God. I didn't take it. Come setch my room.'

'Voetsek from here!' Gittel raved, ignoring Ruth at her side.

Dora ran to her room, crying loudly and bitterly.

'The thief!' Gittel said walking breathlessly up the steps. 'Yesterday she must have heard me tell you where I keep my purse. When I went to my chestadraw just now I found a shilling missing.'

Ruth felt a sick lurch in her stomach.

'Perhaps she didn't take it, Bobbe. Perhaps you spent the money and forgot. Or lost it.'

'So rich I am that I don't know how much money I've got? A shilling is missing I tell you. Go and watch that she doesn't steal anything from the washing line. The dishcloths are still hanging there.'

Waves of nausea flowed through Ruth. She went into the backyard and crept into Dora's room where she was packing her clothes into a cardboard box, crying all the time.

'Miss Ruth, I'm not a tief,' she said between sobs. 'I didn't touch the missis' money. Ai, ai, ai. She said she not pay the month and will call a poleesman. It's a long jenny home. No job, no money. Ai, ai, ai.'

Ruth felt she was choking. This was the first time she had been in Dora's room. It was small, dark and stuffy and smelled of gutted candle and smoke. An iron bed stood in one corner, raised from the floor by three bricks under each foot. Above the bed, on the rough unpainted wall, hung a small unframed picture of Jesus Christ on the cross, with blood streaming from his pierced hands and legs. On the cement floor next to the bed was a large wooden box on which stood an enamel plate with a few crusts of dry bread on it. A chipped enamel cup lay on the floor, next to a broken candle stick.

'My chetch says, do not steal. Jesus Christ,' Dora appealed to the picture above her bed, rolling her eyes until Ruth saw only the whites. 'Jesus Christ, saver, carer for your children, I promist I didn't pinch the money.'

Ruth ran out of the room and came into the kitchen white-faced with distress.

'Bobbe, I took the shilling. I took it to buy chips for Mavis and me. Here, smell my hands. They still smell of chips and vinegar.'

'Leave me alone you silly child. You don't have to feel sorry for that thief. If she can steal a shilling she can empty out the whole house. She must go.'

'Bobbe,' Ruth appealed desperately, beginning to cry. 'I took it. I took it last night when I went to bed and I tied it in my hanky like Bobbe Yenta does. I took it, I took it!'

'Shah, shah! Everything upsets the child. You've got a good heart, mein kind, but Dora must go. She stole the money.'

'I'm going to be sick!' Ruth cried, rushing outside to the lavatory.

Dora stopped wailing. She came to the lavatory door and watched Ruth vomit into the bucket.

'Shame. Po' child,' she said.

When she saw Gittel come out of the kitchen, she fled to her room.

Dovid found Ruth in bed when he came home. She looked flushed and feverish. Gittel told him in a whisper what had happened.

'So I put her to bed and she dozed off for a while but she hasn't stopped weeping all afternoon, repeating that she stole the shilling.'

'Tatteh,' Ruth said weakly getting up on her elbow. 'I did take it. Here, smell my hands. They're still full of chips and vinegar. Mavis didn't have money.'

Dovid sat on the bed and drew her hand to his lips. There was a faint smell of vinegar on it.

'Perhaps she did,' he said to Gittel. 'Perhaps you're accusing Dora wrongly. Why, when anything is missing in a house, do people immediately assume that the shikshe took it?'

'She did,' Gittel insisted. 'I didn't trust her with anything. How many times did she mix up milk and meat dishes? Besides, she's gone already. I didn't want trouble so I borrowed money from Yenta and paid her for the month.'

'If you did take the shilling,' Dovid said quietly when Gittel left the room, 'it was very naughty of you and you must never do such a thing again. But don't worry about Dora. She'll find a job and a better one too. I'd hate to work for your Bobbe if I were a black person. Go to sleep and you'll feel better tomorrow. I'm going to visit your mother now. I'll be back soon.'

'Don't tell her,' Ruth clung to Dovid's neck. 'Don't tell her I took the shilling.'

She cried a little, then asked him to put Zutzke at her feet. As she was falling asleep she remembered the drawing in her case. She gave another sob. That could wait until tomorrow. She would show it to Zeide Berchik before she went to school. Her father did not like mine dumps.

II

*T*he queues at the terminus were long and straggling. It was Wednesday and the shops were shut in the afternoon. Joel pushed his way through the disorderly crowd, looking for the end of the Rand Mines queue which tailed off where the one for Mayfontein began. The first tram was full. On the second, Joel found a seat on the upper deck next to a young miner whose working clothes gave off an acrid smell of damp earth, cyanide and stale sweat. Joel averted his face. He hated public transport with its sweating, weary humanity, its noise and its slow rumbling pace. He glanced enviously at the cars which overtook the tram.

Most of the miners spoke Afrikaans. His father's theory was that land speculation, bad inheritance laws and the resultant poverty on the farms had driven the Boers to the mines. Joel disagreed: These youngsters were simply bored with farm life and wanted the excitement of a city. Some excitement they found: blasting accidents, underground flooding, phthisis, constant competition from natives for the unskilled jobs. He listened to them as they shouted across the tram to one another in their thick uneducated accents. They were large, rawboned farm boys who could hardly read or write and they smelled of the dank underground in which they passed a large part of their lives. Joel was conscious of his own polished, pointed shoes, his immaculate white shirt and the well-cut suit which Dovid had made for him a few months ago.

The trouble with these chaps was that they lacked ambition. All they wanted from life was enough to keep their bellies full and their throats wet.

While Joel disliked the gutteral sound of Afrikaans, he could dissociate himself from it. On the Mayfontein tram, however, he sat in a sweat of embarrassment as the immigrants talked loudly to one another in Yiddish, above the clatter of the iron wheels. He would watch in acute discomfort as an Englishman lowered his newspaper and smirked at the foreign sounds emitted by Joel's co-religionists, as unselfconsciously as though they were still in their shtetl. It was even worse when they trotted out their ridiculous version of English.

Afrikaans simply jarred on his ears. Yiddish, particularly when spoken in public, made him ashamed of being a Jew.

As the tram thundered through the dip, Joel looked into his father's shop. He sat hunched over his workbench, hammering away at a shoe on the last. In the moment it took to pass the shop Joel realised with a pang that Berka had aged: His shoulders were rounded and his hair was grey.

There had been a time when Joel believed his father incapable of ageing or of dying like ordinary mortals. He had worshipped Berka, a tall strong man who told exciting tales about early Johannesburg and about the riotous life on the diamond diggings. He remembered how proud he had been when Berka had borrowed a horse from a mounted policeman and ridden across the veld. Joel and his friends had gaped after him with the same admiration they bestowed on their Saturday morning heroes at the Roxy cinema.

But just as he outgrew the celluloid cowboys, so he began to question his father's values. Where had the exciting life and the fierce pride in his independence got Berka? Was he not, in fact, making a virtue out of his poverty and failure? For the rest of his life he would sit at his workbench, nails between pursed lips, hammering, stitching, patching and glueing. At the end of a day he would return to the dingy house with the smell of other people's dirty shoes clinging to his skin.

Joel pushed aside the image of an ageing Berka. His father had always been more concerned with the Dignity of

Labour, Justice and the horrors of Capitalism than with the welfare of his own family. Joel hated the very sound of those words as he grew older.

Life was far simpler than Berka supposed: If a man had children, he must provide for them. If he found society in a certain state, there was nothing he could do to change it. There had always been injustice, poverty and hardship. It was a tough materialistic world and in order to survive one had to fight it with its own weapons.

Berka could have been a rich man. But instead of buying property in the early days, he had messed about with trade unions and the Yiddish Workers' Club; instead of sticking with Uncle Feldman, he became an itinerant cobbler.

Yet he made Joel feel the failure. What had Berka wanted from him? That he too should buy an ox wagon and trek across the ugly dry veld, dispensing medicine to the boers?

Joel wiped his forehead. The heat and the smell in the tram were stifling. Should he ask the young miner to open a window? He preferred discomfort to contact so he kept quiet.

He loosened his tie and glanced out of the window. Most of the shops were already shut and there were few people in Main Street. As he passed Dovid's workshop he saw Raizel turn into it. An angry flush heightened his discomfort. His father, who was so critical of everything Joel did, did not see what was going on under his own nose. As far as his darling Raizel was concerned she could do no harm.

The tram turned slowly into Rand Mines Avenue. Where it intersected Tenth Street, he saw Sheinka walking along the dusty road, wheeling a pram with Ruth at her side. He felt a momentary stab of anxiety. Perhaps she too was going to Dovid's workshop?

He pulled himself up sharply. From today he was cutting himself off from his family. How they lived and what they did no longer concerned him.

As the headgear of the mine came into view, Joel got up and walked downstairs, breathing in the hot thick air. At least it was not polluted by the smell of unwashed humanity, he thought, jumping off the tram as it clanged to a halt outside the miners' compound.

The midday sun throbbed like a pulse in the pale blue sky. Joel took refuge under a clump of blue gums, wiping his face with a clean white handkerchief. A group of black miners, their naked torsos gleaming with sweat, stood under the trees talking loudly amongst themselves, punctuating their speech with great bursts of amiable laughter.

Such healthy teeth, Joel thought enviously, sucking on a neglected cavity at the back of his mouth. How like animals they were with their shining black bodies and their long rippling muscles. They had no cares or ambitions. He wondered whether they could feel sorrow.

'Middag, Baas,' they greeted him politely, withdrawing to the outer edges of the shade and lowering their voices respectfully.

Joel kept his handkerchief to his nose: the smell of melting tar, sweat and burned meat from the eating house across the road was overwhelming.

He looked uncertainly about him. He had never been to this part of Rand Mines. The Concession Store was smaller than he imagined it to be. It was a square, rain-stained building with a corrugated iron roof and its windows were crammed with a variety of badly-displayed goods, dusty with age. A covered strip of veranda ran along the length of the store and above it hung a rusted sign:

CONCESSION STORE — Naturelle Winkel: Bicycles, clothes, cigarettes, blankets etc.

Adjoining it stood a longer, narrower building with 'Kaffir Eating House' painted in peeling lettering above the wooden lintel of the door.

The source of all Uncle Feldman's wealth, Joel marvelled, wiping his forehead again.

Berka had not exaggerated when he had described the foul smells surrounding the store. On the whole, Joel had discounted his father's tales about his years as an apprentice kafferitnik. He had regarded them as fables designed to teach his children the virtues of self-reliance. For the first time since his talk with Benjamin a few weeks ago, Joel experienced a mixture of doubt and remorse as he looked at the Store, the eating house and the tiny rooms at the back of the store where his father had lived.

It had all sounded so simple, so right while Benjamin was speaking: Uncle Feldman was on the brink of death. He wanted a reconciliation with Berka but this was prevented by his nephew's pride. A man was entitled to decide his own fate, Benjamin conceded to Joel, but did he also have the right to ruin the prospects of his children? Here Benjamin wiped away a tear. If Berka had been more pliant, he continued, Joel and Raizel would have been living in a mansion today and Yenta would not have had to pickle and ferment.

It was diplomacy not deception, he concluded, dispelling the last of Joel's scruples, to visit Uncle Feldman without telling his father. Afterwards Berka would realise that Uncle Feldman meant well by his family and Berka himself would become reconciled with his uncle.

Joel had responded coolly to Benjamin, but as soon as the old man left his room, he flung himself onto his bed in a state of febrile excitement. This was his chance to get rich. Since he'd been working at Hellman's Pharmacy, he had been introduced to the world of the rich. He had been to their palatial homes, sat on their fragrant lawns, dated their beautiful daughters. After a day out it became increasingly difficult to return to Mayfontein, to the narrow life of the immigrant Jewish community. They all seemed coarse and uneducated. He was ashamed of their dress, their speech, their humour and their interminable discussions about Zionism, socialism and petty business problems. With the sophisticated repartee of a tennis party still ringing in his ears, he would greet his parents' guests in a surly manner, in English, then retire to his tiny room to brood over his future.

Now, magically, the future seemed open to him. After his talk with Benjamin, Hellman's Pharmacy suddenly looked small and shabby. More than ever he resented the scraping and bowing to customers. To his mother a pharmacist might seem the source of all medical knowledge in the world. To him Mr. Hellman now appeared as little more than a glorified shopkeeper. He remembered also the indignities he had suffered at the hands of his patronising rich friends. Soon he would meet them on equal ground.

Several weeks passed, however, before he phoned Uncle Feldman. He knew perfectly well that by doing so he was cutting himself off from his father forever. Berka would never forgive him, despite Benjamin's assurances to the contrary.

When he finally phoned Uncle Feldman, the dry rasping voice on the other end had not sounded as welcoming as Benjamin had persuaded him it would. After he had hung up, Joel felt less like a nephew effecting a family reconciliation than a poor relation asking for charity.

Joel adjusted his tie, combed back his sleek oiled hair and crossed the road resolutely. He would make it clear to the old man that he had come at his request and that he wanted nothing from him. His uneasiness, however, increased with every step. By the time he walked into the dark dusty interior of the Concession Store, he felt more lost and uncertain of himself than ever.

And the picture of Berka hunched over his last seemed to have lodged itself indelibly in his brain.

Sheinka walked rapidly up Tenth Avenue, coughing occasionally as the dust thrown up by the pram settled in her tense throat. Her eyes were burning from the hot dry air and every now and again she let out a deep sigh, ending on a drawn out whimper: 'Oy vey iz mir!' Ruth walked beside her silently, kicking a loose stone in front of her.

'Stop it!' Sheinka said angrily, smacking Ruth on the back of her arm. 'As it is I'm suffering from the dust.'

Ruth fell back a few paces.

'Come here!' Sheinka commanded. 'Do you know what you have to do? Knock on his door. If he doesn't answer at first keep on knocking and say loudly: "It's me, tatteh." He'll let you in. When you enter look around to see if anyone is hiding there. If there is, run out and tell me. If there isn't, start to cry, you know how to do that all right. Tell him how unhappy you are because you never see him on half-days any more.'

They turned into Rand Mines Avenue and walked under the plane trees which gave some relief from the burning sun.

Ruth peeped into the pram. The baby was fast asleep. It was unfair. He slept through all this and she would have to do the nasty things.

'I'll wait for you here,' Sheinka said sitting down on a bench at the tram stop. 'And don't be long.'

Ruth crossed Main Street and went into the dark entrance of her father's workshop. She walked slowly up the steps and stood quietly at the door. She heard muffled sounds from within. Perhaps she should run back to her mother and say her father was not in the workshop. Sheinka would not believe her.

She stood with her hand clenched a few inches away from the door, then knocked quickly, once. Silence. She sighed with relief. There really was no one there. With a feeling of confidence she knocked as loudly as she could, several times, then turned the door knob. It was locked. Again there was silence.

'Tatteh!' she called as she knocked again. 'It's only me.'

After a brief interval she heard a key turn in the lock and Dovid opened it slightly, looking down at Ruth from a seemingly great height.

'What do you want, child?' he asked angrily. 'Am I to have no peace even at work? Has your mother sent you?'

Ruth looked at him tearfully and shook her head.

'Then go home. I have a jacket to finish off. I'll come home later. Here's a sixpence. Go buy yourself a pink ice cream from Schumacher's.'

Ruth looked at the sixpence which Dovid held through the slit in the door and with a sudden outburst of tears, she hurled herself against the door and stumbled into the room.

Raizel stood against the rail on which Dovid's unfinished suits hung. The top buttons of her blouse were undone and her hair flowed loosely about her face. Her hand flew to her bare throat and she gasped as Ruth landed on her knees, a few feet away from her. Dovid stood at the open door, unable to move.

Ruth looked from one to the other. She got up, walked unsteadily towards Dovid and began to pull at his shirt.

'You lie, you lie, you lie!' she cried out in English.

She ran blindly from the room, stumbling down the dark staircase. She did not stop running until she reached her mother who was sitting on the bench, rocking the pram impatiently. She threw her head into her mother's lap, gasping for breath and crying loudly. Sheinka looked down at her pale tear-streaked face.

'What happened? Was he there? Was somebody with him? Did he speak to you?'

Ruth felt herself go cold all over and she began to shiver. She pulled away from her mother and sat back on the bench.

'He was there,' she answered dully, watching the melting tar trickle heavily from the iron rails towards the gutter. 'He was finishing off a jacket. He's coming home later. There was no one with him.'

'Dad,' Joel said coming onto the veranda where Berka sat with Hershl and Yenta. 'Dad, I want to speak to you.'

'So speak,' Berka said, lighting up his pipe.

'Privately.'

'Privately,' Berka echoed. 'The time has come at last when my son not only wants to speak to me but he wants to speak privately. Such an invitation I can't refuse. Don't go away,' he said to Hershl. 'I'm sure I won't be long.'

He followed Joel into the lounge. Joel threw himself into an armchair opposite his father and coughed fastidiously when a cloud of dust rose from the cushions. Only a slight tremble in his hands betrayed his unease.

'I saw Uncle Feldman this afternoon, Dad.'

Berka felt his heart contract uncomfortably.

'Dad, did you hear me? I went to Uncle Feldman's Concession Store this afternoon.'

'On business?' Berka asked eventually, his mouth suddenly dry. He cleared his throat. 'Has the old devil started to stock pharmaceuticals in his kafferita?'

'No, Dad. He sent a message to me to come and see him. About a job,' Joel added quickly as his father's face paled.

'He's bought out a dry goods firm and offered me the job of managing it. It's a marvellous opportunity and he wants to make up for the shoddy way he treated you. He admits it. He wants to make peace with you before he dies. He'll give me a share of the profits plus a partnership. On condition that I start immediately, next week in fact. I don't mind giving up my studies . . .'

'Paskudniak! Fool!' Berka shouted as he leaped out of the chair, scattering his pipe and matches. 'Traitor! Your legs should have withered before you crossed his threshhold! You . . . went . . . to his store . . . about a job?' he bellowed incredulously. 'You took a job from that old swine? You filthied your feet by walking into his business? To become his slave? No, it's not true. You're making a cruel joke, Joel, and that's unkind,' he said reproachfully. 'To stab where it hurts most. Too much study has blunted your sensitivities. That's it. In a few months' time you'll be qualified. We, your mother's got money to set you up in business. I'm the fool. Of course you wouldn't throw away five years study. That was a cruel joke, Joel,' Berka repeated as he bent down to pick up his pipe and matches.

Joel rose unsteadily from his chair and put Berka's pipe into his trembling hand.

There was still time. He could withdraw. And be a glorified shopkeeper all his life?

'It's true Dad . . .'

Berka quivered. He stood close to Joel and thrust his powerful short-fingered hands near his face. Joel blinked and held his ground with difficulty. He squeezed his own carefully manicured nails into his palms.

'Look at these hands!' Berka said with controlled rage. 'Look at them. Stained, hardened, cracked and calloused. With work. Honourable work, once I had washed off the stinking entrails and meat from your uncle's kafferita. Your soul will stink like my hands did if you enter his service.'

'Joel, Berka, what's the matter?' Yenta came rushing in from the veranda followed by Hershl.

'Say you're bluffing,' Berka pleaded with Joel, ignoring Yenta. 'Tell me you wanted to punish me for goodness knows what crime I committed against you. Tell me it's not true. The devil himself could not have thought up a worse punishment.'

Joel looked uncertainly from Yenta to Berka.

'Dad, try to understand . . .'

'Out!' Berka roared. 'Out!'

Hershl stepped forward to intervene. Berka looked like a biblical prophet as he towered above Joel, his grey hair awry, his eyes smouldering, his voice cracked and terrible. Joel stood motionlessly before him in his pointed shoes, his thin moustache twitching.

Hershl stopped in his tracks as a painful groan tore itself from deep within Berka. He tried to speak but could not. In a paroxysm of rage and despair he ripped his shirt apart with his work-worn hands.

'Eili, Eili,' he cried. 'Lama azavtani!'

12

'The one at the back, the shiny one, with the cracks. You sure it's got seeds? By me rye bread without seeds isn't rye bread. And lax you've got?'

'Over at the delicatessen, Mrs. Zlotnick.'

'Thanks,' she said taking the bread and turning towards the Passover counter.

'Crazy. Look at them,' she said. 'Six deep, shouting, pushing, grabbing. You'd think there was going to be a famine next week. The lax I'll leave. This place is like a madhouse on Sundays, especially before Yomtov.'

Yenta served calmly behind the Passover counter, unharassed by the clamouring customers. In Berka's slippers she could stand on her feet for hours.

'Take already another box of pletzlach,' she urged the indecisive shopper who was loaded with parcels. 'What you've got is only for one tooth. They're made with this season's apricots, guaranteed kosher for Passover. Mrs. Hirshowitz,' she turned good-naturedly to a fat woman who started guiltily when Yenta addressed her. 'They're fresh, believe me. No need to touch and press. Sorry, Jankala. I didn't have time to make wine this year. The rebbetzin's selling. Try hers. Not as good as mine but guaranteed kosher. Next please! My dear Leib Schwartzman, you don't have to drag the matzos with you. Hershl will deliver in his van.'

'Coming Leib, coming,' Hershl said looking around the kitchen door. 'Go to the cash desk. I'll take your order.'

He returned to the kitchen which smelled of damp concrete. Faigel removed a large tray of cheese blintzes from the oven.

'Careful!' she warned as Hershl approached the tray. 'Use the gloves. You'll burn yourself.'

He was hailed from all sides as he walked down the shop with the steaming blintzes.

'The French loaves will be ready in an hour, Itzik. Go home. I'll bring you one, two — how many do you want? — on my way home. No, Mrs. Jacobs, I didn't raise the price of matzos tuppence a box. The manufacturers did. No pirogen today, Jankala. No time to bake with this rush on,' he said putting the blintzes down on the counter with a sigh of relief. The tray had burned his hands through the towelling gloves.

He was writing out Leib's order when he saw Mrs. Pinn striding purposefully towards him. It was too late to retreat into the kitchen. He stretched himself to his full five foot four and smiled politely.

'Fluxman's sell salt herrings at sevenpence,' she hissed. 'Yours are eightpence.'

'Then, my dear Mrs. Pinn, you must buy them from Fluxman.'

'They haven't got any at the moment.'

'Ahah! When I haven't got herrings I sell them at five-pence.'

Hershl turned to Leib who was grinning delightedly.

'Leib, I warn you. If Chaya hears rumours that you're buying Faigel's blintzes, you'll be thrown out of the house. A divorce you can get for such disloyalty,' he added, pointedly ignoring the indignant Mrs. Pinn who glowered at him before storming out of the shop.

'You're the only one who can handle that Gestapo bitch,' Leib said with admiration. 'Such scathing politeness. But be careful. She'll discover a mouse in your bread and report you to the health authorities.'

'She can go to . . .' Hershl mumbled looking towards the counter where Yenta was working cheerfully. He wondered that Mrs. Pinn had the gall to come into the shop at all.

By two o'clock the shop was quiet again. Hershl sat down behind the cash desk and lifted his feet onto the cross bar. That's where he felt his increasing weight most, on his feet. He ate too much and had no exercise. It was years since he had ridden his bicycle. He patted his stomach critically. It would do him good to miss lunch today. He usually did on Sundays. Faigel went home at one to eat with the boys and he remained on with a few helpers.

'See you at four,' he called to the counterhands who were taking off their light blue overalls which he had made obligatory wear. 'Be back in good time for the afternoon rush.'

He beamed when he saw Yenta coming towards him with a steaming cup of tea in one hand and beef on rye in the other.

'Yenta, you're spoiling me. I'd just decided not to eat lunch.'

'And make yourself sick? Denks Gott you're healthy. A little paunch doesn't matter. It makes a man look prosperous. Brisk today, eh?'

'It always is before the festivals. Yentala,' he said looking down at her slippers through which her big toes were protruding. 'Berka needs a new pair of slippers.'

'A klog! I forgot to change. Fancy walking down Main Street like this. Behind the counter nobody sees,' she said hurrying away.

A remarkable woman. Hershl watched her bow-legged progress towards the kitchen. Perhaps all women were strong in adversity. She had grieved for a week after Joel left home, then dry-eyed but gaunt she came to him with her proposition. She had two hundred and seventeen pounds in her Post Office savings account. She was as strong as a horse. Were these sufficient qualifications to buy herself a small share in his business? If not, she had others: Nobody, as Hershl knew, pickled cucumbers like she did. Her gefilte fish was outstanding. She knew five different ways to prepare herring. For the Festivals she would make taiglach, pletzlach ingberlach. All she wanted was a small salary and one day, please God, when the business was paying well, she would take a proportionate part of the profits. Money was secondary: she needed an occupation.

'What'll I do with money? Buy myself a chemist shop? A new house Berka doesn't want. A dowry for Raizel I won't need . . . Anyway, it's a gamble and as dog racing shows no profit, I'll try business. What do you say?'

With Yenta's money and with loans from the millers Hershl had remodelled Sharp's Delicatessen. He installed wall fittings, added another refrigerated counter and put down a new floor. Then he leased the shop next door which he converted into a bakery. He engaged another baker and several apprentices. Dirk managed the bakery. In his newly-acquired van which he drove with unwarranted confidence, Hershl delivered bread all over the city. After the Passover, however, he was taking on a permanent vanman as he himself was needed in the shop.

Hershl stirred his tea thoughtfully as he looked around the shop. It was more than a shop; it was an institution. And not in the way Leib meant either. My sales assistants may be elderly or unfortunate but they're loyal and hard-working, he rebuked Leib who said that Sharp's had become an old aged home. What's more, they create a homely atmosphere.

At first only he, Faigel and Yenta had worked in the shop. Then Sara Sher's husband died, leaving her destitute. Hershl put her behind the bread counter. When Gershon Green's business in the country failed, he gave him a job at the delicatessen counter. Werner Neuberg, a refugee from Germany, was in charge of the meat department. In spite of his volatile moods and the shake in his hands, he was a genius at smoking and pickling meat. The demand for his products had become so great that Werner was training an apprentice butcher. In addition to this permanent staff, a host of widows and other needy women came in to work on Saturdays and on Sundays when the shop was busiest.

On these days people came from all over Johannesburg to buy hot bread and delicatessen and to meet people whom they might not have seen since they landed in Cape Town. Old friendships were renewed over smoked lax and pickled herring; new ones were created in the free-for-all discussion that arose among strangers. They stood around the counters and in the passages, parcels in hand, talking about old times and new occupations; about the world situation and the Nazi threat. Hershl thought of leasing Leib's old smithy when he moved out in a few months' time, and converting it into a tea room where everyone could debate in comfort. He would call it 'The Diet', and engage a Chairman, not a Manager.

He smiled at his fantasies. He was well-pleased with the success of his business though it left him with insufficient time to go to synagogue on Friday evenings. In spite of all this activity, he never lost sight of his ultimate goal: to settle in Palestine with his family.

'If I forget thee, O Jerusalem,' he chanted wistfully, wishing that his days in the Diaspora were already over.

He had little to complain about. The boys were growing into fine reliable lads. Moishala was in his first year at High School and Joshua would join him next year. Daniel was well-settled in school and Faigel had stopped agitating about moving out of Mayfontein.

Their next house, God willing, would be in Zion.

'Hershl, I've taken some smoked fish and a few blintzes for Berka's lunch,' Yenta said as she came out of the kitchen. 'It's as well that he hardly notices what he eats these days. Poor man. He's taken it hard. I'll be back at four. Finish your sandwich, Hershala. You'll need strength for the big rush.'

Berka had taken it very hard. Hershl saw him towering over Joel . . . Ach, it was too painful to recall. Perhaps if he, Hershl, had spoken to someone about the conversation he overheard that night between Benjamin and Uncle Feldman, this irreparable rift between Joel and Berka might have been averted. Over-delicacy could be as disastrous as Mrs. Pinn's obsessive nosiness.

Berka had barely adjusted to his break with Joel when that shattering incident with Raizel occurred. Hershl sighed. It was his fate to be witness to all Berka's heartbreak.

One evening after a long tiring day in the bakery he and Yenta had walked home together. It was a cold night and the air was full of smoke from a veld fire. As they approached

Yenta's house they heard shouting and crying from within. Berka rushed out at that moment with a wounded cry, followed by Raizel who was sobbing.

'Nachas from children!' Berka shouted, his voice thick with drink. He thrust a piece of paper at Hershl. 'Here, read this.'

'You should know what everyone in the suburb knows,' Hershl read, reluctantly. 'Your daughter Raizel is having an affair with Dovid Erlich. If you want proof, watch his workshop on a Wednesday afternoon.'

Berka snatched the note from Hershl and staggered off in the direction of Dovid's house, followed by Yenta who was wringing her hands.

'Come!' he commanded when Raizel lagged behind. 'Once and for all we shall learn the truth.'

By this time all the neighbours had come onto their verandas, hugging their jerseys around them. For a while Hershl stood helplessly at Berka's gate, then went home. A short while later Berka strode blindly out of the Erlichs' house, followed by Dovid who rushed like a madman towards Mrs. Pinn's house. He dragged her out from behind the lace curtains, onto the veranda where in full view of the astounded neighbours, he slapped her across the face. She ran from neighbour to neighbour shouting hysterically:

'You're a witness! You're a witness! You saw him hit me.'

But the frightened neighbours had apparently seen nothing and heard nothing and Mrs. Pinn's threatened action for assault came to nothing. And from nothing, Hershl mused, even Mrs. Pinn could not make a court case.

Faigel tried several times to tell him what 'they' were saying, but Hershl sternly forbade her to repeat the gossip of the suburb. All he knew was that Berka had withdrawn from the community. He gave up his work on the Refugees' Fund, his own creation; he visited none of his old friends; there were no more talks on his veranda, no poker games, no impromptu suppers at his house on Sunday evenings.

After a while he forgave Raizel but Dovid, like Joel, had died for him.

Gittel and Yenta continued to see one another regularly and on Friday evenings they still walked to old Weinbrin to fetch the 'Yiddisher Americaner.' Ruth visited Berka only at his workshop: Sheinka had forbidden her to go to the house.

At first Berka had avoided Hershl, but the latter persisted in his visits to Berka's workshop, ignoring his deliberate rudeness. While Hershl spoke to him Berka hammered away at his last in silence. One day, however, when Hershl was speaking about the situation in Europe Berka broke in bitterly:

'What hope is there for humanity as a whole when on a personal level sons betray fathers and friends deceive friends?'

From then on the stone on Berka's heart was lifted and contact was re-established between him and Hershl.

'I'm at home with the Boers,' he answered when Hershl taxed him with his withdrawal from the Jewish community. 'They're simple, open-hearted people, narrow but honest. You know where you are with them. If they call me a bloody Jew I give them a bloody nose. They don't bear a grudge and neither do I. But with our Jews it's different. They greet me with solemn faces and pretend nothing's happened. But behind my back they whisper and they judge. They've made Raizel's life a misery.'

The rhythm of life in First Avenue had been broken and Hershl mourned its destruction. He could not bear the aridity which had followed on Berka's misfortunes. On Friday evenings Hershl sat alone on his veranda, waiting in vain for the play to begin. But the stage remained in darkness as though in sympathy with the tragedies being enacted on a larger scale in Europe.

Hershl felt out of tune with the world, guilty: amid chaos and destruction his own life ran smoothly. But at least it gave him strength to help others, especially Berka. Hershl drew him out of his private hell and talked to him of world affairs. There was plenty to talk about in those dark years of impending tragedy, nineteen thirty-eight and nineteen thirty-nine.

In China there was war, though the Japanese were retreating; in Spain, Franco was making a final thrust to the Mediterranean and the government forces were all but beaten; in Russia the mock trials and the real executions continued; in Palestine there were riots and massacres. And Chamberlain, that umbrella-carrying hypocrite, was running like an errand boy to Hitler with peace offerings. He reminded Hershl of Joel — he did not tell Berka this — with his moustache and his false smile. In the interests of 'peace' he was sacrificing people and lands that were not his to dispose of. While Hitler made a triumphal entry into Austria, he wrote notes of protest. After the Anschluss nobody was safe. The Germans massed on the Czechoslovakian border and wherever Hitler went the persecution of Jews followed.

'If Chamberlain hopes to satisfy that voracious monster's appetite,' Hershl told Berka, 'with titbits of Austrians, Slavs, Czechs and Jews I, Hershl Singer, no great politician but not a fool either, can inform him that he is making a big mistake: the monster will swallow him up as well, umbrella and all.'

'And who will listen to Hershl Singer?' Berka asked, taking out the nails from between his lips. 'Only Berka Feldman. And mainly because he's a captive audience behind his last and in danger of swallowing nails if he argues.'

The whole world went deaf and blind while Jewish judges were thrown out of their jobs in Vienna; students forced out of universities by Storm troopers and Jews thrown into jail and deprived of their livelihood. Jewish merchants were made to stand outside their own shops, some of them the greatest and most famous in Vienna, with placards around their necks reading: 'Do not buy from Jews'. Shops were daubed with stars of David and Hitler Youth offered protection by installing themselves in the shops and purloining the takings.

And names like Sashenhausen, Dachau and Buchenwald were appearing in the newspapers. The atmosphere was heavy with foreboding.

Daily the queues outside the foreign consulates in Vienna grew longer and more desperate. The Swiss announced that they could not take in refugees without means of subsistence; other countries followed suit. And Jews could leave Austria and Germany only by impoverishing themselves. There was an average of a hundred suicides a day among Austrian Jews. Hershl understood but abhorred these suicides.

'Let them die fighting, protesting, not by their own hands,' he said to Berka.

'Hershl Singer sits behind his cash desk in Africa and lays down what the Jews in Austria ought or ought not to do,' Berka said. 'What would you do if a gang of Greyshirts or Blackshirts burst through your doors one day, beat you up, smashed your shop to bits, then sent you off to a concentration camp in the Free State without letting Faigel know? Would you die fighting and protesting? How would you defend yourself? Pelt them with blintzes?'

One had only to read the daily papers to realise that Berka's was not such a wild fantasy. The Malanites and the Greyshirts were competing with one another for the honour of being the best and sincerest anti-semites in the country. Hershl himself was prepared to give the prize to Wiechardt of the Greyshirts, but Malan himself was no mean Jew hater. He could get the consolation prize because he had given the Jews some consolation: At an election meeting early in 1938 Malan had said that for their own good the Jews should not press for increased immigration. They knew as well as he that as soon as Jews constituted more than four per cent of a population, the Jewish Question arose. He personally would not discriminate against the existing Jews in South Africa, but if more came in, he would not be able to give this assurance.

The less intrepid Jews in the community began to resent the refugees: their own security was being threatened. Hershl hated their self-interest but he understood their fears. Swastikas were appearing all over Johannesburg, synagogues were being defaced and Nazism was openly supported in certain quarters. The children from the German School, for example, had been given a holiday to celebrate Hitler's victory in Austria. The Nazi salute had been taken and Heil Hitlers had punctuated the Principal's speech. He prayed to God to bless the Fuehrer and took a personal pledge of loyalty to him.

Hershl recalled the talks which he had had with Berka and Dovid in the early thirties. Assimilation is the only answer to the Jewish question, Berka insisted. That's what the German and Austrian Jews are unsuccessfully trying, Hershl argued; a Jewish state is the only solution. You're both wrong, Dovid said in his dreamy fashion: Socialism is the answer. Only then will there be true brotherhood of men. National, religious and social differences will automatically fall away and men will live in peace.

By 1938 Hershl no longer knew the answer, and he and Berka no longer talked in grand generalities. The pressing reality of every day life had been more than they could cope with.

Hershl sighed as he wiped the crumbs off his chin and walked to the entrance of the shop. It was a bright sunny day but there was already an autumn chill in the air. Main Street was quiet. Soon its peace would be shattered by spluttering motor cars which would disgorge whole families onto the sidewalk, all of whom had come to buy hot bread and Werner's wursts and dahr-fleisch. The children made straight for Schumacher's ice-cream shop. By the time they returned to Sharp's, however, the ice-creams had been eaten and they hung around the counters while the motherly assistants fed them titbits of meat, pickled cucumbers and pastries.

'Eat, eat, my child,' they urged.

Hershl watched Aaron Blecher's car come up the hill. He was early today. That meant he wanted to talk to Hershl before the crowds arrived. Hershl shook his head sadly. What could one say?

'My good friend,' he shook Aaron's hand warmly. 'How glad I am to see you. But if you've come to talk politics, take your custom elsewhere. I'm not in the mood. Tell me instead what you've named your new block of flats. Your good wife wanted to call it Minsidman Mansions if I recall correctly, after your children Minnie, Sidney and Herman. Have you persuaded her to use a more euphonious name?

No? Don't be disheartened. As long as the flats face north and the rental's reasonable, you'll have no trouble letting them, even if you call it Hamentashen Heights. A good name? You may use it. Come inside. We've got time for a cup of tea before the rush begins.'

13

*A*n icy wind swept through Main Street, picking the plane trees bare. The leaves whirled wildly about, scraping drily against the pavements and the shop fronts. Berka turned up the collar of his greatcoat and walked slowly up the hill. His eyes watered from the cold and from the acrid smoke which hung in the air after last night's veld fire. All night long it had raged through the dry grass and in the morning the veld lay black and devastated under a shroud of frost. Throughout the day it had smouldered fitfully and now, in the purple dusk, isolated pinpoints of fire still glowed in the veld.

The smell of warm bread enveloped Berka as he walked past Hershl's new bakery. In the old days he would carry a warm bread home with him, but since Yenta had gone into business with Hershl, he rarely went into the bakery.

He pulled his cap over his forehead and increased his pace. He could not bear the muted tones and the grave looks with which his old friends greeted him. He preferred the brutal directness of his barmates.

'Your dandy son kicked you in the balls, eh?' someone said soon after Joel left home. 'Never mind. It could've been worse. Mine's serving a stretch.'

They could say what they liked, Berka thought, as long as they didn't mention Raizel.

The sound of laughter and singing from the bar could be heard a block away.

> Bobbejaan klim die berg,
> So hastig en so lastig,
> Bobbejaan klim die berg . . .

121

Berka pushed open the swinging doors. The bar was full of miners who had just come off shift. Some of them sat in the far corner, singing lustily. The others crowded around the counter. Jan Burger, his young neighbour, was among them. He had a pint glass in his hand and was looking pensively into the distance. Chidrawi waved to Berka from one of the tables.

'Bernard my friend, come and join us,' Arthur Campbell called as Berka hung his coat and cap on a buck's horns. 'We're celebrating my retirement. This round's on me.'

The group of English-speaking officials made room to include Berka in their circle.

'Thirty years we've known one another,' Campbell said putting his arm around Berka's shoulders. 'Remember the first time we met? If Llewelyn hadn't separated us I'd have given you a bloody nose for calling me an Englishman.'

'Who knew the difference between a Scotsman and an Englishman in those days? To me everyone who spoke English was an Englishman. Before you met me did you know the difference between a Polak and a Litvak?'

'I certainly know it now. Polish Jews talk Yiddish like Cockneys talk English and Litvaks can't distinguish between an 's' and a 'sh'. Same on you, you shilly boy! Only the Russian Jews speak Yiddish correctly.'

'Right! Now this round's on me. Campbell, you've got a Yiddishe kop. In fact, you're half a Yid.'

'Feldman, so are you!'

They laughed heartily and slapped one another on the back. By the time they reached the sixth round the other officials had drifted away, leaving Berka and Campbell to their reminiscences.

'They call this a bar,' Campbell said scornfully when John the barman moved out of earshot, 'and that hulk of flesh a barman. Do you remember the old Mayfontein before it burned down after the '22 Rebellion?'

'Do I remember it! Thick blue gum beams on the ceiling, a carved wooden bar . . .'

'The huge fireplace with copper pots and pewter mugs . . .'

'And Tiny Tim, all six foot four of him, lording it behind the counter . . .'

'Aye, that was a man. He didn't need that rifle he kept under the counter. He could knock two heads together like, like . . .'

'Like kids cracking nuts on Pesach,' Berka added.

'Just so. The men were men in those days, eh Bernard? Nor were they afraid of dying for their convictions. Remember the Fordsburg Rebellion?'

'Do I remember! The workers in the trenches, the police on the mine dumps . . .'

'The People's flag, is deepest red . . .' Campbell intoned sonorously, above the combined efforts of the singers in the corner.

'Vat jou goed en trek Ferreira . . .' they sang drowning Campbell's solitary voice.

'We had them worried for a while.'

'But what can you do against tanks and planes? Even if their aim wasn't so good.' Berka chuckled. 'They missed the trenches and hit McIntosh's grocery store, poor devil, and the Wesleyan Church. Like toys those De Havilland DH9's looked, spluttering in the hot summer sky.'

'Bernard my friend, the workers weren't with the Council of Action, that was the trouble. "Workers of the World Unite!" the Council pleaded, but the rank and file wanted the white workers to unite against the black workers. The Council wanted to do away with the colour bar in industry and social life, but the lousy scabs said, "kaffir work for kaffirs, skilled work for the whites". It couldn't work.'

'And their other slogan, "Do you want your sister to marry a kaffir?" They always came up with that one. What did they think the Council of Action was, a marriage bureau?'

'There will never be a true white proletariat in this country,' Campbell said sadly. 'It's the blacks that'll make the revolution and I'm not waiting around for it, Bernard. Next month I'll be home again.'

They finished their drinks in silence. The miners were now singing in a more nostalgic vein.

My Sarie Marais is so ver van my hart

Maar ek hoop haar om weer te sien . . .

Berka joined in. Fields of mealies, mud-walled farmhouses, thorn trees. dried up water holes rose to his mind and he felt close to the Boers again. Campbell was right about many things, but he had never understood the real Afrikaners. Berka did. This was his home, these were his people, his songs. Unlike Campbell he did not have home to return to; unlike Dovid he did not pine for der heim. Neither could he share Hershl's mystic feelings for Palestine. But he felt uneasy about Pirow, Malan, Wiechardt . . .

> . . . O bring my terug na die ou Transvaal
> Daar waar my Sarie woon,
> Daaronder in die mielies by die groen
> doring boom,
> Daar woon my Sarie Marais . . .

He loved it all, the good with the bad. And in winter when the veld burned down he knew that with the spring rains the green shoots would come up again. It rarely destroyed the grass roots.

Campbell was right. He was only half a Yid and he was glad of it.

'. . . brave men,' Campbell's voice suddenly intruded on his ears. 'Spendiff and Fisher shot themselves rather than give up. And all those fine chaps were shipped Home after the Rebellion. They really knew the score. These fellows here,' he looked around the bar contemptuously, 'are Union men like I'm Chairman of the Chamber of Mines. All they care about is protection from black competition. White trash, that's all they are,' his voice rose aggressively. 'Landless yokels, ignorant Boers . . .'

'Campbell!' Berka said reproachfully, 'I'm surprised at you. Such intolerant talk. These men are our brothers, our fellow workers.'

'They're certainly not my brothers. They're the brothers of the Commandos who shot at the workers . . .'

'Quieter, Campbell. At our age we can't get involved in bar room brawls. You can't generalise like that. Think of Scheepers, think of . . .'

'You think of them if you want to. And the hell I can't generalise. Have you heard their public pronouncements? Strutting little Hitlers, every one of them. For them the battle of Blood River is still raging and the Boer War's only just begun. Even that man Burger who works on my shaft is absolutely blind to any ideas that didn't originate in the laager. And he's quite intelligent. Call him over. Hear for yourself.'

'Leave him, Campbell. I've spoken to him often, he's my neighbour,' Berka protested. 'I've met more enlightened Afrikaners in my time and so have you. Remember . . .'

'Call him over. He won't come if I do. He's typical, I tell you. I work with them all day.'

'Jan, join us for a drink,' Berka called reluctantly. Jan was sitting at a table with Chidrawi.

Jan looked suspiciously at Campbell, then back at Berka who smiled reassuringly at him. He drained his glass and with a slight swagger, walked across to the counter.

'We're discussing the colour bar, Mr. Campbell and I,' Berka began. He did not feel like arguments that evening. 'We, er, were saying . . .'

'Mealie-mouth!' Campbell cuffed Berka affectionately. He turned sternly to Jan. 'We were saying that the white workers banded together to protect their interests against the black workers and not against the exploiting mine bosses. We believe that the black man must be trained, organised into unions and that if he is, he won't undercut the white workers. Together they can get a good deal for the working class. There's work enough for everyone. Don't you agree?'

Jan flushed deeply and pushed his drink aside. Campbell had baited him before.

'I say that if we teach the blerry kaffirs skilled work, we'll be out of jobs. Anyway, those bobbejaans can't learn skilled work. They've just climbed out from the trees and lost their tails. They're fit only for kaffir work. In the Bible it says about hewers of wood and drawers of water . . .'

'What did I tell you?' Campbell turned triumphantly to Berka. 'Even their humanity is denied. Bobbejaans in trees. Well, well. I must be off. I'll drop into the workshop before I leave for home, Bernard my mate.'

He nodded curtly to Jan and walked away.

'Those blerry Englishmen,' Jan spat out. 'I hate them.'

'He's Scotch,' Berka corrected.

'These blerry Englishmen think they own the world.

They come here, make trouble, then go back to England, leaving us with the mess.'

'He's right about the black workers, Jan. Black and white must unite against the white bosses . . .'

'Ag nee, Oom. They're savages. It's every white man for hisself. I'm a Union ou all right but I'm not a commie. We trekked from the Cape because the blerry English tried to make us equal. And we fought the kaffirs for the land and we won. If they'd won, we'd be dead. They're still alive. This is our home. I haven't got another home like Campbell.'

'You've got a poyerse kop, Jan. Do you know what that is? A terrible affliction. You just don't understand.'

'Ag, I understand all right. If I don't want the kaffirs in my Union, I'm an onderdrukker. If I want protection from the black bastard's cheap labour, I'm not tolerant. You've told me that before. And if I don't like Bolshie talk, I've got a poy-whachacallit kop. Oom, if I listened to you, the kaffirs would sit in Parliament and I'd be doing the kaffir work. And don't forget, I know the bastards. My voorvaders were slaughtered by them at Weenen. You can't trust them.'

'My voorvaders were slaughtered by God-fearing Christians in the crusades and in pogroms, and I'm still speaking to you. We live in a different world today, Jan. We must be tolerant.'

Berka suddenly wearied of the conversation. It was hot and stuffy in the bar. He felt his own tolerance ebbing.

'Jan, your friend Chidrawi who seems drunker than usual, is calling you. Perhaps we'll walk home together later on and talk some more.'

He took his drink and walked to a table near the door. The crowd in the bar was thinning out. Those who remained looked as though they had settled in until closing time. The miners in the corner were still singing. As the evening drew on, their songs had become increasingly nostalgic.

O Boereplaas, geboorte grond,
Jou het ek lief bo alles.
O moedertaal, soetste taal,
Jou het ek lief bo alles.
Al dwaal ek ooit
Die heel wêreld rond . . .

Berka hummed the tune then stopped, puzzled. He heard it before, that very evening, yet he knew that the miners had not sung it. 'Boereplaas' usually came towards the end of their repertoire, by which time they were soaked in nostalgia and booze. Where had he heard it? His head felt muzzy and he could not remember.

Suddenly he thumped on the table and laughed out aloud. Of course. Campbell had sung it. The melody of 'Boereplaas' and 'The Red Flag' was identical! The conservative Boers and the Revolutionaries had used the same tune for their most sacred hymns.

Another five minutes and he'd go home. Time enough to go out into the cold night. What was there to rush back to? Yenta was at work; Raizel was sad and silent; his friends treated him as though there'd been a death in the family, and in a sense there had been: If he were a religious Jew he would have sat shiva for Joel. Berka's eyes misted. He had never been so lonely; not when he had lived in that tiny room at the back of the kafferita; not when he had travelled over the empty veld with only his voorloper and his thoughts for company. Never.

Ruthie was his only comfort. In some indefinable way they were linked by loneliness. Yet why should she be lonely? She was doing well at school; she had a friend; she was drawing beautifully. The wall next to his work bench was already half-filled with her pictures of the veld, of the mine dumps, of the blue gum plantation. Her English had improved. These days she spoke English to everyone except to him and to Gittel.

That's it. Why did it make him so sad that she spoke English to everyone? Even to Dovid. It had something to do with her loneliness. He pondered this strange fact deeply but found no answer. Somewhere there was a link but tonight he was too drunk to find it.

He was so lost in thought that he only became aware of the argument behind him when Jan and Chidrawi stood in the centre of the room, facing one another angrily.

'But what did I say that was so terrible, Jan? And why are you defending her? I'm not the only one in Mayfontein who says so. Everybody . . .'

'Shut up, you lousy Arab. If you open your blerry mouth again, I'll donner you up.'

'Mrs. Pinn told me herself. And all I said was that I always knew she was a sexy bit from the way she handled the cucumbers in my old shop . . .'

Jan's fist shot out and with a moan Chidrawi sank onto the floor, clutching his stomach.

Berka looked around in bewilderment. Everyone turned away from him in embarrassment. Jan came up to his table and helped him up.

'Come, Oom,' he said gently. 'It's time for us to go home.'

Jan helped him on with his coat and together they walked out of the bar. The wind had died down and the stars shone brightly in the clear dark sky. The veld was burning quietly in the night and the sky mirrored the sparks with icy stars.

'What if the grass roots are burned, will the grass never grow again?' Berka mumbled. 'Look, Jan, how dark the sky is, how cold the stars are . . .'

'Don't worry, Oom, it'll be all right.'

Jan grasped him firmly under his elbow. Several times Berka's knees buckled under him. He looked back sadly at the bar and knew that he would never enter it again. His world was shrinking daily.

Neither he nor Jan spoke on the way home. It was only when they reached his house that Jan patted him awkwardly on the shoulder and said:

'Please don't worry about it, Oom. They've all got a lot of dirty mouths.'

Berka drew in his breath at the musty smell in the passage of his house. Although Yenta no longer made wine and cucumbers, the smells lingered on in the passage, like memories of old times.

14

'It's black, it's black,' Berka sighed looking at Raizel over the top of the Sunday paper. 'This war will make all others look like Purim parties.'

Raizel smiled at him absently, glanced nervously at her watch and turned back to her knitting. Knit one, purl one, she mouthed. How many anguished days had she knitted into garments, a tear a stitch, an ache a row. Her father's jersey should cry out in agony from the pain of its creation. Empty, emp-ty, emp-ty, the needles had clicked rhythmically in the days following that dreadful night. Bitter, Bit-ter, bit-ter, they tapped on as she made a cardigan for Yenta, a jersey for Berka, a dress for herself, clothing them all in her misery. Only now as she knitted a pullover for Jan did she feel a sort of peace.

The first few months had been torture for her. Hostile stares followed her to and from work each day. 'Home-breaker!' one woman had shouted while her husband smirked in a shame-faced manner, loath to associate himself with the crude attack, yet aroused by Raizel's apparent availability. At work she sat like an exhibit in her glassed-in office while customers bought their packets of pins and measures of ribbon, and peered inquisitively at her. 'Shameless hussy', they said smugly to one another.

She did not know which was more painful: the open hostility or the prurient curiosity of her friends. Her instinct had been to run away but Berka dissuaded her from it.

'If you leave,' he said, 'the Mrs. Pinns of this suburb will have gained an easy victory. They're the evil ones, not you. You simply erred.'

Her bitterness and resentment grew daily. Had she succeeded as a homebreaker, life might have held out some promise. As it was, it stretched before her like the dry empty winter veld. She might have coped more easily had she not seen Dovid. Working in the same street, living on the same block, it was inevitable that they should meet though several weeks passed before they did for the first time.

As she walked wearily out of Nathan's one evening, she came face to face with him. They stood for a few moments looking helplessly at one another, unable to move. His face was white, his eyes red-rimmed and he looked like a wraith from another world. Her heart contracted painfully. The memory of warm summer evenings and honeysuckle; of tailor's chalk and steamed cloth overwhelmed her as she stood trembling at the door of Nathan's Drapery Store.

"Betrayer!" Berka had shouted while Sheinka collapsed in hysteria. Yenta and Gittel clung to one another and Ruthie, apparently unconcerned, played in a corner with Zutzke. Tell them, Dovid, Raizel had pleaded with her eyes. Tell them that you love me, that your life with Sheinka is over, that we're going away together. He remained silent, rooted in anguish, while his very life blood seemed to seep out of him. Not a word did he say to protest his love for her.

'I must speak to you,' he said as they stood at the entrance to Nathan's Drapery Store. 'Please meet me some-where.'

'Leave me alone, Dovid Erlich,' she said, retreating into the doorway. 'I don't ever want to speak to you again. You smell of Vicks and carbolic soap. I hate you.'

'Knit one, slip one, pass slip stitch over,' she murmured in agitation, her heart pounding at the memory of that meeting.

'Did you say something Raizel?' Berka looked up from the newspaper.

'No Dad, I was following the pattern.'

'The world is falling apart and she sits and knits,' Berka grumbled.

Raizel glanced up involuntarily at the yellow patch on the wall where Dovid's wedding photo had hung. She smiled scornfully when she remembered the gold-rimmed glasses on his nose. False, like his intellectual pretensions, like his avowals of love. False, like the literature he had foisted on her. Lies, the lot of it. People did not die of love. They lived on from day to day with the bitter taste of ash in their mouths. In real life Anna Karenina would not have thrown herself under a train. She would have bought a ticket, boarded a train and returned to her husband. She would have grown fat and ugly and sat about, waiting for nachas from her son. Raizel looked at her watch again.

'Expecting someone? Going somewhere?' Berka asked.

'Perhaps,' she answered defiantly.

'You've changed, Raizel,' he said sadly.

'So have you, Dad. I remember when you used to bring Jan to the house. Now you're barely polite to him.'

'There's an old Yiddish saying, Raizel, that the innkeeper loves the drunkard but not for a son-in-law.'

'You're so pious these days and so fond of Yiddish sayings,' she scoffed, but her hands trembled as she knitted.

When the full implication of the bar room fight had filtered through to Berka he was shocked and angry. He did not need Jan to defend his daughter's honour. She, on the other hand, was touched by the gallantry and the gaucherie. Her knight in miner's gear. At least he defended her. Dovid had denied her.

Jan became a regular visitor to the house and she accepted his offerings of marigolds and wild kosmos from the veld. Berka received him with mixed feelings. He did not want to encourage the friendship between Jan and Raizel, but he did enjoy Yenta's discomfiture. He also enjoyed provoking Jan into political arguments.

'Ag, your father doesn't understand,' Jan told Raizel. 'My grandfather had to plough with one hand and shoot kaffirs with the other. After the Boer War he lost his farm and his children became bywoners on a stranger's farm. We nearly starved. We lived like kaffirs on the land. So my father came to town and worked as a labourer and here he had to fight the kaffir in another way, for a job. I'm sick of it, man. Wherever I turn I'm called a bloody Boer; they laugh at my English and say Afrikaans is a bastard language. I want to have my own farm, my own life, like my grandfather had before the War. The Boer War they call it. It was the English War. Do you understand how I feel?'

Raizel understood. That, and many other things. When Jan talked about turning the red soil and planting mealies in the spring, he wanted her to be there. When he spoke of a little house under bluegum trees, he wanted her to share it. She listened to his dreams as she had listened to Dovid's songs and tales, only now she was part of the dream. She looked beyond Jan's clumsy frame and found a vulnerable human being.

Berka was elated by old Burger's distress over his son's friendship with the Feldmans.

'Verdomde Jode!' they heard the old man bellow through the thin kitchen wall.

'That's me,' Berka would smile. 'Old Burger is losing his hold over Jan. I'm weaning him away from his volkskultuur.'

'And throwing him at your daughter,' Yenta said bitterly.

'Rubbish,' Berka had said. 'Raizel's too sensible to fall for a Boer like him.'

But when he saw that Jan and Raizel were growing closer to one another his attitude to Jan changed abruptly. An open attack would have alienated Raizel so he used more subtle means. With the practice acquired from years of debating with Dovid and Hershl, he enmeshed Jan in complicated arguments and verbal traps out of which the perplexed man could not extricate himself with dignity. His forehead would wrinkle painfully as Berka's irony pierced him, exposing his muddled thoughts and eliciting a response so poor in language and content that Berka read both repugnance and pity on Raizel's face.

But Berka misread the proportion of repugnance to pity. She leapt to his defence and drew closer to Jan. I should have encouraged her to leave the suburb when she wanted to, Berka thought as he looked on in helpless frustration.

Raizel enjoyed the scandalised stares she drew when she and Jan began to court openly. With him at her side she felt strong and protected. In the eyes of the community she was ruined beyond its wildest expectations. A pregnancy in one so immoral they might have expected, even hoped for, perhaps forgiven, but to flout their most sacred unwritten law — 'thou shalt not consort with goyim' — was unforgivable.

Only Yaakov Koren, the other outcast in the suburb, greeted her sympathetically. Thus he had been hounded when he divorced his wife in Lithuania and married the widow Kagan. Raizel often saw him wandering distractedly around the dam, peering into its acidy depths as though looking for a solution to his problems.

Only once had she encountered Dovid when she was walking with Jan. The experience had been so painful that for a while it had taken the joy out of her defiance.

Her parents, of course, presented a different problem. She was reluctant to hurt Yenta, to deprive her of that crippling nachas which Jewish parents exacted from their children in return for having brought them into the world. But Raizel was determined to make her own life, even if it hurt her mother. At worst, Yenta would grieve for a week, as she had done for Joel, perhaps less in her case, then throw herself into her work at Sharp's. She was a strong woman.

As for Berka, let him now practise what he had preached to her all her life: tolerance.

As she sat in the lounge waiting for Jan, however, Raizel felt apprehensive. Perhaps they should have waited. She got up and looked out of the window. It was a beautiful autumn afternoon, but a cold wind had arisen in the south and was lifting the mine dust like a veil above the dumps. She would not miss this dry windy season when she finally left Mayfontein. In the country autumn would come slowly, graciously, as Jan had described it, revealing itself in the subtle change of colour in the veld and in the blue cloudless skies. There at least, one would not see the dumps and the headgear wherever one looked and there, perhaps, she would find a measure of peace at last.

The dust, the dust, Yenta sighed as the wind blew up Main Street, ruffling her dyed hair, exposing the grey at the roots. It burned her eyes, stung her nose, lodged between the roof of her mouth and her dentures, rubbing blisters into her gums. She stopped for breath at the top of the hill. Below her the houses lay huddled together, enclosed by the city on one side and the dumps on the other.

This was Berka's great big beautiful world from which he and Raizel had refused to move. In the last few years it had become a dust-ridden prison for them all. But she had a plan. If it worked Raizel would be with her cousin Sorrel in Durban within the next few months, away from her past humiliations and her future dangers.

And this time she knew she would have Berka's support.

Tolerance, Berka had preached all his life. And what was more, it had to be his special brand of tolerance where goyim were as good as Jews and kaffirs the equals of white people. For his own family he had shown precious little tolerance. She could understand his threat to throw Benjamin down the nearest mine shaft if he ever appeared in Mayfontein again; she could understand his loathing for Uncle Feldman (he should rest in peace, one spoke no ill of the dead). But that he should not forgive his only son, that was beyond her comprehension. Raizel he had forgiven readily enough and God knows, there was much to forgive her for. But when Joel had rejected his heritage of hate, Berka had driven him from the house. Out of their lives, Yenta thought bitterly, pushing her hair out of her eyes. She shivered: these autumn winds cut one to the bone.

So Joel had worked for Uncle Feldman. Could Berka have made him a better offer? So he had not finished his studies. Did that prevent him from marrying a rich girl and from becoming a director?

After Uncle Feldman's death some months ago there had been a picture of Joel in the newspaper. 'Young director appointed to the board of Feldman Holdings' the caption read. He had looked so distinguished, so handsome, Yenta recalled with pride. She had put the paper on Berka's chair and found it torn into little pieces.

Berka would have preferred Joel to fail rather than to be proved wrong.

She had not seen Joel for almost two years. In the beginning he had phoned her occasionally. When she suggested meeting him he said: It will hurt Dad. She knew her Joel.

Below that cold exterior was a warm heart. He had not asked her to his wedding because he was afraid of causing conflict between her and Berka, not because he was ashamed of his family as Raizel claimed. Raizel should only show such consideration for her parents.

Hershl was the only one of their friends who had seen Joel since he left home. He had gone to Joel's business to collect for the Refugees' Fund.

'He's broadened out,' he reported to Yenta, evading her question about the size of his donation. 'And he's got a very smart office. On the door, in golden letters, is written Joel M. Feldman, Director. I didn't know he had a middle name.'

'Morris,' Yenta lied. 'After my late father's late brother, the one who was studying to be a rabbi when he was carried off with brain fever, may he rest in peace.'

He was all right, her Joel. She had nachas from him even if it was from a distance. And now, thank God, it seemed as though she had found a solution for Raizel as well.

'Find a nice little drapery shop,' she had written to her cousin Sorrel, a wise kindly woman who lived in Durban, 'and I will help you buy it. Money I've got. Write to Raizel when you're ready and offer her a partnership. She knows the trade well and is a good steady worker . . .'

Sorrel had found a business. One part of the match was therefore arranged. Now she would work on Raizel.

She heard voices from the lounge. That yoven from next door was here again. Like a Cossack he looked with that huge body, red face and blond hair. A fine drinking companion for Berka; an even better suitor for Raizel.

She would be the death of her, that girl. One scandal barely blown over and she was starting another. People were beginning to talk again and that witch Mrs. Pinn still stood behind her lace curtain, watching, listening, waiting.

'Dad,' she heard Raizel say, 'You're being unfair. Jan's only saying that the white worker must protect himself against the black's cheap labour.'

Defending him again, Yenta raged, walking into the lounge.

'I've brought you some lunch,' she said to Berka. 'Oh hello, Mr. Burger. I didn't know you were here again for a

135

change. Here, Raizel, go warm up the blintzes for your father's lunch.'

'I've eaten,' Berka said brusquely, annoyed at Yenta's appearance at this stage. 'I ate two hours ago, at lunch time. Raizel fried polony and eggs. But by all means warm up the blintzes for tea,' he called after her as she stalked out. 'Jannie likes them even better than koeksusters, don't you, my boy?'

Jan was confused by the sudden change in Berka's tone: a few minutes ago he had attacked him bitterly. His surprise, however, was short-lived. Berka leaped into the attack again the minute Yenta left the room.

'You've never left the laager,' he continued. 'Kaffir work! What's kaffir work? That's why you've never built up a strong white proletariat, that's why you've got a class of poor un-employable whites. Have you never heard of the dignity of labour? Look at these hands! I've never been ashamed of what you call kaffir work. You should hear Hershl Singer on the subject. You Afrikaners could learn something from the Zionists about the dignity of labour.'

'Learn from the Jews about work?' Jan asked incredu-lously. 'That's a new one. All they know is how to buy and sell and make profit. Them and the coolies. Why don't they go back to Palestine or Russia? Or they're blerry capitalists draining the blood of poor Afrikaners, or they're blerry kaffir-boeties!'

'Ahah!' Berka got up from his chair, pale and furious. 'In anger the truth comes out. Did you hear him, Raizel? Did you hear what he said?' he demanded.

'You're different, Oom Bernard. You said yourself that you're only a Jew in name. I've never seen you go to the synagogue. And you said yourself that you were a true South African. Nothing else.'

'I'm a Jew, damn you! And whenever I try to forget it someone like you reminds me. I'm a Jew like all those others who're being killed in Europe today. I'm the verdomde Jood your father rants about behind that kitchen wall. And you're a bloody chatas!'

Jan stood up and looked helplessly from Raizel to Berka.

'I'm sorry, Oom, what I meant . . .'

'Chatas, chatas, chatas!' Berka shouted at him. 'Next time you'll be telling me that some of your best friends are Jews. And then you'll ask me if I want my daughter to marry a kaffir. I've got an answer to that one: I'd rather let my daughter marry a kaffir than a bloody chatas. And now get out! Voetsek!'

'Dad!' Raizel placed herself between Jan and Berka. 'Have you both gone mad? It's nothing, Ma,' she turned to Yenta who came rushing into the lounge. 'Leave us alone. It'll only complicate matters. Please.'

'Nothing? It sounds like a pogrom to me!'

'Please ma, later. I promise I'll talk to you about it later.'

'Poyerse kep all three of them,' Yenta muttered as she left the room, reluctantly. She did not want to antagonise Raizel now.

Jan moved towards the door. Berka stood in the centre of the room with his braces hanging down from his waist, breathing heavily. His face was pale and his left eye twitched uncontrollably.

Raizel propelled Jan out of the room into the dark passage.

'Go now,' she whispered urgently. 'I'll speak to you tomorrow.'

'Tell him now,' Jan demanded. 'I'm sick of everything, of all the lies and the hiding away. I'll tell my father tonight and we can leave for Rhodesia next week. I've got enough money.'

'Not now,' she pleaded. 'Please be patient a while longer. I'll tell him but not now.'

Berka was standing where she left him. Raizel took him by the hand and led him to the sofa. She put her head on his shoulder and he stroked her face gently. For a while they sat in silence.

'Older but no wiser,' he said eventually as his breathing slowed down. 'Older, lonelier, more unsure. You think you're sure because you're young, Raizel. When I was young I lay in in the forest while the Cossacks murdered my family, and I cried out to the black empty sky: "If there is a God let him strike me dead!" So I knew there was no God and I put my trust in men. When they failed me I cried: "Eili, Eili, lama azavtani?" I was reproaching the God I didn't believe in for forsaking me. How can one live without faith in God, without faith in men? I am utterly, utterly alone.'

'You're not alone, Dad. Everyone loves you.'

'Like they love an idiot child. Poor Berka, they say. They pity me for the loss of my son, they pity me for my drunkenness; they pity me because I'm losing my daughter to a goy.'

Raizel drew away from him. The tears streamed unchecked down his leathery wrinkled face into his bushy moustache.

'I know, Raizel, I've known for a long time.'

She put her hands over her face. She longed to deny it.

'It's my fault. I didn't teach you to be a Jew. I brought him here. But I've tried to show you he's not for you. I ridiculed him and you pitied him. I saw it. You were moved by his tales of hardship, by the struggles of his people, by his pathetic bouquets, just as you were by Dovid's songs . . .'

'Don't talk about Dovid!'

'You don't love Jan, you don't belong to his world any more than you belonged to Dovid's. You must find your own world. I understand Jan, I even like him. When he spoke about the Boers, I saw the veld again, smelled it after the rain, watched the cold wind blowing through the grass that bent and swayed like Jews at prayer. I remembered the marvellous sense of solitude in which I revelled because I knew it would end. Now my solitude is real, unending . . .'

'Dad, listen to me . . .'

'. . . because I denied what I was. Tolerance,' he laughed bitterly. 'That's the prerogative of gods, not of man.'

'Dad, I can't bear to see you like this . . .'

'Don't go with him, Raizel. Stay with your own kind, inadequate as they may be. You'll never be one of them. They won't let you. You've seen their thin frightened women with curlers in their hair, scrounging around for credit after their husbands blow their wages on drink and on the dogs . . .'

'Jan's different, Dad. He's a good man. All he wants is a plot of ground, a cow, a few chickens. When all my good Jewish friends turned away from me, he was my friend.'

'He'll call you a whore later.'

'For that he's got a precedent, Mary Magdalen.'

'Then he'll call you a bloody Jewess and for that he's got plenty of precedents.'

'He won't, Dad. I'm converting.'

'You're — converting?'

'Don't look so shocked. To you it doesn't matter to what God the superstitious pray. And I've got to have a God. You killed the Jewish one for me.'

'In these days you're talking about converting? When they're hunting down Jews like wild animals, robbing them, killing them? Did you hear what Jan himself said just a few minutes ago?'

'You don't understand Dad. I have to belong to someone, to something. I don't know who I am any more.'

'Don't do it, Raizel.'

'I'm not converting out of cowardice, because I'm ashamed or afraid of being a Jew. I simply don't know how to be one any more. And that first day I walked into the dark cool church, not Jan's church, and saw the statue of the mother and child in the candlelight, folded so lovingly in one another's arms, some forgotten memory leaped up and I felt at peace again. Please try to understand Dad.'

She threw her arms about Berka's neck and wept bitterly. He drew her tenderly into his arms and stroked her hair, whispering:

'Shah; shah. Shah; shah.'

No other words would come. His mouth felt full of dust.

15

*D*ovid let the handbills slide out of his hand onto the polished stoep.

'I decline with thanks,' he composed in his head, 'your invitation to a riot.'

He got up and paced out the length of the stoep. Two and a half long steps, four shorter ones, the size perhaps of a prison cell. But then he had the hinterland of home beyond this, a prison of more insidious dimensions. From the bathroom he heard Sheinka crooning a Yiddish melody for Phillip. She had put aside her Vicks bottles and clutched the child to her chest instead. She refused to recover completely, however. When he went to the Anti-Fascist meetings, she lay on her bed in the darkened room with vinegar compresses on her brow.

'Those Blackshirts will kill him, the hero,' she would wail. 'Shushide he wants to commit, a man with his responsibilities.'

On the other hand, Dovid reconsidered, he would accept the invitation, even if it was to a riot.

He looked with distaste at the potted geraniums along the ledge, then towards the dumps where the sun was setting. A mild breeze rose from the south, nudging the heavy pink clouds across the sky.

There was no sign of rain: The meeting would take place.

It was inevitable that it should. 'Afrikaner Girls Kicked by Jews'; 'Jewish Hooligans Assaulting Our Girls', the Afrikaans headlines had screamed after last week's meeting. Leib, an eye witness, had a different story to tell.

He and Dovid had gone to a meeting in the City Hall to protest against the latest Nazi atrocities. In the crush they had been separated. Dovid got into the meeting and Leib joined the overflow outside the City Hall. Squashed into a doorway, Dovid listened to the Archdeacon and an Afrikaans professor condemn the Nazi outrages. They were alien to Afrikaner culture and tradition, the professor said, warning South Africans to guard against the intrusion of Nazi ideas.

The Chief Rabbi appealed for a place of refuge for the homeless Jews of Europe.

Out in the streets, however, there was chaos and dissension. In the midst of the unruly mob David saw Leib tearing apart a banner with a swastika on it. He interrupted his task only to swing out at an attacker. Dovid pushed his way through the mob and managed to propel the protesting Leib towards the tram terminus.

'When we couldn't get into the Hall,' Leib told him on the tram, nursing a cut cheek, 'we decided to have our own meeting. It was peaceful until two men and a girl marched towards us, waving a banner with a swastika and shouting "Heil Hitler!" The crowd went beserk. As we moved towards them a group of their storm troopers appeared and the battle was on. The police did nothing until we got the upper hand. Then they moved in. I wonder how many of our boys landed up in hospital.'

Dovid bent down and picked up the handbills from the stoep. One, written in Afrikaans, called for an anti-Jewish protest meeting that evening at seven thirty. 'Forward!' it concluded. 'There's a fight to fight!'

Dovid reread the other, issued by the South African Anti-Fascist Movement. He had helped to distribute them, reluctantly. The sentiments were impeccable but violence, which he abhorred, was bound to follow.

'Citizens, workers, trade unionists! Hitler's agents
in South Africa — the Blackshirts, Greyshirts,
Nazis and Fascists — have called a meeting in
Johannesburg (City Hall Steps) on Thursday,
November 24, 1939. They have instructions from
Nazi Germany to start pogroms and concentration

camps in our land. Are you going to stand by and see Nazism start this butchery in our country? NEVER! Then come in your thousands to a mass meeting to condemn Nazi terrorism in South Africa, this Thursday evening, November 24, at 7 p.m., City Hall Steps to demonstrate your abhorrence of Hitler's methods in Johannesburg. NOW. Before it is too late. Down with Inquisition Methods in South Africa.'

They would come, those fascists, with their bicycle chains, loaded piping and knuckle dusters, perhaps with knives and guns. Dovid had never overcome that sick feeling in his stomach as both factions moved towards one another. All he did at meetings was to shout 'Down with Hitler!' in answer to their 'Down with the Jews!' The thought of smashing his fist into a human face made him nauseous.

'I'm no hero, believe me,' Dovid had assured Sheinka when he limped into the house with Leib the previous week. 'My only injury is a twisted ankle acquired in the act of running away from a policeman's truncheon. But we must protest. Like Leib says: "Open your mouths! Don't let them shit on your heads!" '

'But why you? Why Leib?' Sheinka cried, incensed by Dovid's bantering tone. 'Why not Weinbrin's son or Steinberg's big brutes? You're a married man, with a family to support.'

Dovid crumpled up the handbills angrily and smashed his fist down on the veranda ledge, throwing over a potted geranium. He winced with pain. If those bastards wanted a fight they'd get it. He walked into the house to fetch his jacket.

'You're going somewhere?' Sheinka asked as she came out of the bathroom carrying Phillip in a large bath towel.

Dovid still smarted with humiliation over his son's name. Sheinka had refused to call him Yehuda, after Dovid's father. Phillip, she called him, after Faivel Meishe, Gittel's revered uncle.

'Put him down,' he said brusquely. 'He's big enough to walk.'

'I asked if you were going somewhere, for a change,' Sheinka replied holding Phillip closer. 'What's it this time?

A jacket to finish off? A Workers' Club meeting? An Anti-Fascist demonstration? Anything, as long as you can get out of the house.'

'As a matter of fact the Prime Minister's invited me to advise him on the international situation.'

'So, don't tell me.'

'I know where you're going,' Ruth whispered to Dovid when he came into her room. She was sitting at the table drawing on a sheet of rough black paper. 'You're going to fight Hitler on the City Hall steps, now, before it's too late. I read the paper. I can read nearly everything but some words I didn't understand.'

'Everything she knows,' Dovid said with a mixture of pride and alarm. 'Don't say anything to your mother for heaven's sake. She'll . . .'

'I know,' Ruth replied calmly. 'She's afraid of pogroms. When I was little I also was. Do you remember?'

She had drawn closer to Dovid in the last few months but continued to speak English to him.

'How do you like my drawing? On that ox wagon is Zeide Berchik. You can see his moustache. The grass is high because it's summer and there's been lots of rain.'

'If there's been lots of rain, why is the grass grey?'

'Because Zeide Berchik is all alone in the veld. He says that he's not so sure any more if he'll reach a farmhouse before dark. So I made the grass grey. Grey is lonely.'

'Do you see Zeide Berchik often?'

Ruth looked towards the door and lowered her voice.

'Oh yes. Two or three times a week, after school. He waits for me then we go to Ron Davis's for chips.' She blushed and turned away. 'We eat them together in his workshop. Don't tell Mommy. When I was small Zeide Berchik told me there wouldn't be any more pogroms but I don't think he's so sure any more. I tell him not to worry. Daddy, he said I mustn't say he said it but that I should tell you not to go to meetings on the steps any more. He says they'll split your head open and that anyway you haven't got so many brains. He was joking. About the brains I mean.'

'Daddy,' she added, suddenly tearful as he moved away. 'Why don't you sing any more?'

'Why don't you speak Yiddish to me any more? Why am I "Daddy", not "tatteh" any more?'

'Because, because I'm big now and it's easier to speak English.'

'So you see, people change. But I'll sing for you any time you like.'

He kissed her again, took his jacket off the hallstand and walked quickly out of the house. He was due to meet Leib at the tram stop in five minutes.

They sat on the lower deck of the tram. A crowd of noisy miners occupied the top deck. Leib pointed his thumb upwards.

'Our playmates for the evening,' he said.

The sun had set but the buildings beyond the Dip still reflected, on their steel and glass, the rosy glow from the west. Main Street was quiet. How strange and empty it felt, Dovid mused, as they rode past Nathan's Drapery Store. Smaller, dingier, like a place revisited after many years' absence. Raizel had run away with Jan Burger to Rhodesia. Yanke was installed in Chidrawi's fruit shop and Chidrawi himself had become a wholesale fruiterer on the market. The Pinns still sold second-hand junk together with gossip and slander, and in Steinberg's butchery, the flypaper still hung from the ceiling black with victims.

Only Hershl's bakery livened up Main Street. Late shoppers were leaning over the counters, buying the hot bread and the pickled meat for which Hershl had become famous in Johannesburg.

'Some people have got it and others haven't,' Leib sighed looking at his smithy. 'I don't begrudge Hershl his good fortune, but as a neighbour for so many years, a little bit of it should have rubbed off onto me.'

'Set fire to your smithy and claim insurance,' Dovid advised.

'The only inflammable thing in there is my furnace,' Leib said ruefully. 'Anyway, if I'm a schlemazel I'm in good company. Berka isn't exactly a roaring success. Nor are you. You're still at your old Singer, turning out works of art and struggling for a living, while that trouser-maker, that haizenschneider, Yaakov Koren has just opened up a trouser factory.'

'He'd have done better to open up a shirt factory. Black-shirts, greyshirts; he'd make a fortune.'

'It hasn't made him any happier,' Leib said. 'Since his marriage to the widow Kagan he looks darker and gloomier than ever.'

'He's got his wife and children on his conscience.'

'Don't you believe it,' Leib said. 'It's probably because he has to pay his workers too much or because the black widow spider is eating him up. Anyway, I'd rather be rich and unhappy than poor and unhappy. As long as I'm healthy . . .'

'You won't be healthy for long if you keep going to these meetings,' Dovid said sharply. 'And why I schlepp along I don't know. This isn't my country. Why should I fight its battles? I should be in Europe, in a direct confrontation with the Nazis.'

'This is direct enough,' Leib said looking upwards.

The tram clattered through the Dip, past Berka's darkened shop. From his workshop window Dovid often saw him walk slowly up the hill, stopping for breath more frequently than ever. His shoulders were stooped and even his moustache seemed to droop wearily. Dovid was glad that Ruthie saw him often.

The tram clanged to a halt outside the Library and the miners shuffled down the iron steps. Many of them were still in their working clothes. Others, with beards grown for the Centenary celebrations, wore Voortrekker dress. They streamed off the tram towards the Library gardens.

'That's where they're massing,' Leib said. 'And from there they'll march to the City Hall steps. Look at them. Thick as flies on Steinberg's flypaper. Four hundred of them if there's a man. They've come in from all the mining towns on the Reef. I wonder where they're hiding their lead piping.'

Dovid's stomach lurched. If he had to die or be injured, he wished it could have been for a better cause. He did not take these Nationalists seriously and did not believe, as Leib did, that South Africa was seriously menaced by Fascism or by anti-Semitism. The Nationalists had enough on their plates with the black people. A wave of dizziness swept over him. He closed his eyes and saw the flushed triumphant face of Jan Burger.

'Come on,' he said angrily. 'If they want trouble we'll give it to them.'

People were coming in from all directions towards the City Hall. Dovid greeted some acquaintances from the Jewish Workers' Club and together they walked in silence around the back of the City Hall, past the Municipal offices towards the square where several hundred people had already gathered. The Committees stood on the steps under a red banner: 'Join the United Front Against Fascism.'

Leib nudged Dovid.

'Look at the police. They've surrounded the square. Those truncheons look ugly to me. I wonder if they'll use tear gas?'

Dovid disliked Leib's morbid interest in violence. He looked nervously over his shoulder towards the Library Gardens. A murmur of excitement spread through the crowd as the clock on the Post Office tower struck seven. As the last chime died away there was an expectant silence. But the meeting did not begin.

'It's seven. What are they waiting for?' Dovid asked.

'For them.'

The sky had grown darker with clouds which were floating in from the south. Too late for rain, Dovid thought as he heard the sound of singing in the distance, interspersed with shouts and cheers. As the marchers drew nearer Dovid heard snatches from 'Sarie Marais'. The crowd around the steps grew silent and tense as the marchers' footfalls were heard. Then suddenly they appeared, about twenty abreast, carrying banners with anti-semitic slogans.

They waved to the police and jostled against the silent demonstrators as they took up their positions. A bearded man leapt onto the steps and shouted in Afrikaans:

'God is on our side in maintaining Christianity in this country!'

Boos and cheers greeted his statement. The meeting had begun. Dovid stood at the edge of the crowd trembling with rage at what could be heard of the speaker's anti-semitic tirade. Most of it was drowned by the booing and the singing of the anti-fascists.

'The People's flag, is deepest red . . .' they sang while the Greyshirts broke in with 'Die Stem'.

The crowd was swelling with people who were still streaming in from all sides. Dovid was no longer on the periphery, but trapped in the centre as it swayed and quivered like a wave about to break.

'Slay the Christ killers!' a voice screamed.

Dovid lashed out wildly in an effort to move out of the centre of the swirling mob. A heavy face with puffy eyes and dark wavy hair thrust itself to within inches of Dovid's face. On the breath of tobacco and liquor the words 'Jood! Bangbroek!' were spat into his face. Two short vicious punches landed below Dovid's ribs, winding him and replacing fear with uncontrollable rage. He lifted both his fists above his assailant's head and rained down blow after blow.

'Kill the redhead! Die rooikop!' he heard behind him.

As he turned a sharp heavy object hit him on the temple. The post office clock chimed and flashed across his vision and the flag above the steps fluttered briefly before his eyes as he fell underfoot, amid the screaming, the singing and the blowing of police whistles.

'Strap him down. Put up the sides. He's threshing about so wildly, he'll fall off.'

Dovid struggled to get out of their grasp but firm hands held him down. His knees felt weak as he looked over the edge of the headgear. Cyanide tanks, tube mills, the sun like an evil eye. The dam smelled of chloroform and the stone crushers pounded and beat in his brain until he was breathing in unison with them.

'Help, help!' he called to the black men below the headgear, far, far away, but they did not move. He was lashed to the great wheel and the ropes cut into his flesh. A warm trickle of blood ran down his face. Slowly the wheel began to turn. The ground, the tanks, the dumps rose towards him. Around and around it spun until he lost consciousness.

'You're all right, you're all right,' a soft voice said at his side. He put his head against the sofa to smell the perfume of her hair. He coughed and drew back. Disinfectant. He struggled to rise, to open his eyes but fell back, exhausted. A sharp pain shot through his head and he saw Sheinka lying on the sofa, crying. Berka, distraught and pale, stood beside Raizel.

'Betrayer!' he shouted. Dovid stood in the middle of the room while his soul, a little golden bird from the song, escaped from his body and flew away, high above the head-gear.

> Wie ken ich in finstern wald,
> Fargessen die liebe zu dir,
> Dermon ich mir dein gestalt,
> Ervekt zich a veitik in mir . . .

'Say something,' Raizel pleaded with her eyes. 'Don't deny me. Tell them, Dovid. Tell them we love each other.'

He looked beyond her eyes to the grey grass that was growing along the river. His mother and father walked beside a loaded cart, casting fearful glances at the burning village behind them. His brother Meishke called to him from the other side of the river.

'Be brave, the fire will purge us of all our narrowness. We will emerge stronger than ever,' he said.

'I'm not a coward, I'm not a coward!' Dovid called out to Raizel. 'Don't go away. Life turns to dust without you. Raizel, Raizel, I love you!'

Dovid opened his eyes painfully. A high white ceiling arched over his head. He turned his head and saw a strange woman in white sitting beside him.

'This is a hospital?' he asked. His tongue felt thick in his mouth. He raised himself painfully onto his elbow. His right hand was encased in plaster and he felt the tightness of a bandage on his head.

'Yes,' the nurse replied crisply. 'And if you're to recover quickly, stop threshing about like a lunatic. We had to strap you down in case you injured yourself. You'll be all right. A few broken ribs, a crushed hand and a cut on the head. You get what you deserve when you make riots.'

Dovid looked around him, dazed. He was in a long ward in which there were at least twenty beds.

'Hurwitz from the Workers' Club,' a cheerful voice introduced itself as the nurse walked away stiffly.

'Of course,' Dovid turned around painfully. 'What happened?'

'We gave as good as we got. They're in another ward in case fighting breaks out again,' Hurwitz smiled. He had his arm in a sling. 'Broke it on a poyerse kop. And I got a knife wound in my side.'

'I remember very little. I must have been knocked out at the beginning.'

'Things got rowdy and the police, as usual, showed restraint until the anti-fascists got the upper hand. About fifty people were injured, theirs and ours. Young Kofsky from Springs was shot in the chest. He'll be all right though. Our Yiddish boys gave them a good go. When the police dropped tear gas bombs, the crowd moved off along Eloff Street. They say the fighting continued until eleven at night. At least we fight back now, not like in the pogroms when we bared our throats.'

Dovid sank back wearily onto his pillows. He sat up suddenly and asked:

'Leib Schwartzman! What happened to him? We went to the demonstration together.'

'He's all right. He came to visit you yesterday with your wife,' Hurwitz replied, 'but you were delirious. You sang love songs and you shouted and asked why the grass was grey. Then you cried a little — it's not a disgrace — and took your wife's hand like Robert Taylor does in bioscope, and said "I love you, Raizel." You'd think a woman would appreciate a romantic gesture even if it was made in a delirium. But no. Up she jumps and flies out of the ward. Women,' he sighed. 'There's no pleasing them.'

16

'*D*ovid! Russia has invaded Lithuania!'

Gittel hurried into the lounge with the 'Yiddisher Americaner' in her hand. Her cheeks were flushed and her glasses quivered at the tip of her nose.

Dovid put down his book and smiled indulgently at her. Since his mishap on the Town Hall steps fifteen months ago, they had grown closer. It was Gittel who had nursed him when he came out of hospital. Sheinka withdrew from him completely, and Phillip became the pivot of her existence. She clung jealously to the child and would allow neither Dovid nor Gittel to draw near him.

'Shvieger,' he said patiently, 'that happened in June 1940, the news is seven months old. In addition, it is incorrect. Russia was asked by the Lithuanians to protect them from the Nazis, they did not invade the country. It's time you changed from the "Americaner" to the "Afrikaner". At least the local Yiddish press is topical, if biased. If you carry on reading the American paper not only will you get the wrong information but you won't even know when the war is over.'

Gittel opened up the paper.

'Here, let me read it to you: "This is all part of the Nazi-Soviet Non-Aggression Pact, a true misnomer if ever there was one. Aggression Pact it should be called, for the two totalitarian giants have cut up Europe between them. Stalin guards the back door while Hitler invades Poland, and now Russia, with Hitler's blessing, takes over Lithuania. What will be the fate of the Jews in these two countries?" '

'All lies,' Dovid said. 'The "Americaner" is a reactionary anti-Soviet paper. Russia had to sign a non-aggression pact with Hitler because the Western Powers would not come to an understanding with her. She had to survive. But that doesn't mean that Russia is really Hitler's ally. It's just political strategy.'

'I don't understand politics but I'm worried about the Jews,' she said. 'In the First World War the Russians sent us into exile because we were too near the frontier with Germany and they said that Jews were traitors. Onto cattle trucks they loaded us and deep into Russia we travelled . . .'

'Don't worry, shvieger,' Dovid interrupted. She forgot that he too had been part of the exodus from Ragaza. Gittel was growing old. 'Don't worry, the Jews will be all right. In fact,' he said wistfully rubbing his right hand which had not completely healed, 'Lithuania will now enter a golden age. Jews, Christians, workers and peasants will live together like brothers; the wealth of the country will be redistributed and a new era will begin. More than ever I long to be there. A bloodless revolution! My brother Meishke has realised the dream of a lifetime.'

'Well,' Gittel said doubtfully, 'it doesn't say all that in the "Americaner". And a wise woman like Miss Breen would not write for a paper that told lies. By the way, have you heard from your family lately?'

'No. But I'm sure they'll be all right now. I envy them. To be living in a true socialist state!'

'And your hand, Dovid,' she said hesitantly. 'I've seen you in pain, often. Why don't you give up your workshop? I hear Yaakov Koren has offered you a job as works manager in his factory. You wouldn't have to use your hand . . .'

'I'd rather starve than work in that sweatshop,' Dovid said brusquely, turning back to his book.

Thus dismissed Gittel walked out of the room. Berka would explain the Russian invasion. He had cleared a wall of Yenta's pictures and pinned on it a large map of the world. Every night he listened on the wireless to a man from London — the miracle of it — and then made marks on his map. He knew what was happening all over the world.

Gittel dragged her swollen feet heavily along the pavement. I'm growing old, she muttered to herself. Her eyes were worn out with watching for the postman; her gallstones bothered her; the buzzing in her ears had worsened and lately her feet had swelled badly. See a doctor, everyone urged. She, however, had confidence in Brown the Chemist. Your swollen feet are from your heart, he told her, and he should know. It was a good profession, a chemist. Brown was loved and respected by everyone. Joel too might have been respected had he become a chemist. Instead people were saying that he was even meaner than Uncle Feldman. Not to have asked Yenta to his wedding. A heart of stone the boy's got.

As for Raizel, she always knew she would come to a bad end. Not that anything had happened since she ran away with that goy (a terrible fate in itself), but Gittel was expecting to hear bad news at any time. Miss Breen insisted that mixed marriages ended in tragedy.

In the meantime Raizel was writing cheerful letters to Berka and Yenta. They had had to forgive her; what could they do? How she could be cheerful on that farm in Rhodesia, living with a raw boy, surrounded by black people, Gittel could not imagine. And to think of all the rabbis in their family. They would turn in their graves if they knew that Yenta would be the grandmother of a little chatas. That was nachas for you.

Count your blessings Gittel, she counselled herself. At least your daughter married a good Jewish man. So he isn't such a marvellous provider. If Sheinka had married a goy, God forbid, he would have beaten her to death long ago. As for her son Chaim Leib, at least he was healthy, even if he didn't write from America.

She hurried past the Burgers' house. No need to run past, she remembered as she looked into the garden which was choked with weeds. Only the honeysuckle had survived, perfuming the whole street. The Burgers had moved out soon after Raizel and Jan fled to Rhodesia. They had opposed the marriage as strongly as Berka had, even though Raizel had converted and probably wore a large cross over her heart. Opgeschmat, converted. Bitter, bitter.

There were more goyim than Jews in First Avenue these days. As the Jews moved out, they moved in. Mrs. Zaidman and her daughter were in Yeoville; the Zlotniks, the Pearlmans and the Weinbrins (it was so hard to get the 'Americaner' these days), had moved to Greenside, and even Leib Schwartzman and his family were leaving Mayfontein. He had bought a little motor spares business in Germiston.

'From horses to horseless carriages,' he said. 'So long I remain in the transport business.'

Had her family moved out of Mayfontein earlier . . . What was the use of speculating? The damage was done. With Raizel's departure the tension had eased. Even Mrs. Pinn was quiet. Berka claimed she had no time for local politics because she was working for the Gestapo. The ideas that man had.

Gittel waved to Faigel Singer who was standing on her veranda, all dressed up, ready to go collecting. After Hershl built the new bakery she had stopped work and was elected chairlady of the women Zionists. The Singers now mixed in the highest circles. Why people in their position still lived in this dusty mining suburb, Gittel could not imagine.

'Good morning, Gittel,' Berka said cheerfully as she walked into the house. 'What brings you here so early on a Sunday morning?'

'I've forgotten. I'm growing old, Berrala. Where's Yenta?'

'Since she became Manageress of the new shop she's a changed person. I hardly see her. And with her new false teeth and her blue-grey hair I wouldn't recognise her if I did. But at last I've got my slippers back, holes and all. Do you know Gittel, she looks better now than she did as a young woman. Some people are born middle-aged and gradually grow into it.'

Gittel dismissed his remarks with a wave of the hand. It was shameful though the way Yenta neglected her home and Berka. He lived on smoked meat and polony from the shop. She hadn't cooked a meal in months.

'So early in the morning,' she looked disapprovingly at the glass of beer in Berka's hand.

'My medicine,' he said, 'without which I could not conduct the war. It's good for despairing hearts, desolate souls and foul tempers. Just as you hug to yourself your hot water bottles when you get a gallstone attack, so I pour down a couple of these and everything is cured at once. You should try it.'

'Russia has invaded Lithuania,' Gittel said, remembering why she had come. 'I know you know. Dovid said it's old news. But I want to know why. Dovid says one thing and the "Americaner" says another.'

'Greed, madness,' Berka answered promptly. 'A crazy need for power. Here,' he said digging into a file which he kept near the map. 'Look at this picture I cut out of the paper. Molotov, Von Ribbontrop (zol arop zein kop) and Stalin signing an agreement on the partition of Poland. Bandits, the lot of them. Look at Stalin. Like a cat who's had a saucer of cream. Dovid believes everything they say in Moscow. He's remained a slave to his old ideas. I, my dear shvegerin, think independently.'

'And the Jews? What will happen to the Jews? The "Americaner" says there are three million Jews in Poland and 200 000 in Lithuania. God alone knows what will happen to them.'

'Then leave Him to care for them. There's nothing we can do,' Berka said casually but a pained look passed over his face. 'Come, shvegerin, let's bring you up to date. Have a look at my map here . . .'

When Ruth came into the lounge she saw Gittel seated in an armchair and Berka standing in front of the map, like a school teacher.

'. . . and so you see how black the situation is. Not only have Czechoslovakia, Poland, Denmark and Norway fallen to the Nazis, zollen zei varbrendt veren, but they've overrun Holland, Belgium and Luxemburg as well. France has fallen and now they're getting stuck into the Balkans. There's fighting in Yugoslavia and in Greece. Hello, Ruthie. Come in, my sweetie. Join my class on global warfare.'

'Daddy's also got a map but not such a big one. And Mommy won't let him put it onto a wall. Bobbe, I've reached the heel but I don't know how to turn it,' she said handing over a half-finished khaki sock to Gittel.

'Cripples the soldiers must be to wear your socks,' Gittel said looking critically at Ruth's knitting. 'Long in the leg, short in the foot, one foot bigger than the other. But she tries,' she told Berka. 'At school the children are all knitting for the soldiers up north.'

'And of course there's the war in North Africa,' Berka added. 'Well Gittel, nothing they write in the "Americaner" will surprise you again. You're up to date. Ruthie,' he said kissing her on the forehead. 'I always said you'd be as straight as a bluegum and as pretty as kosmos. Like Greer Garson you'll look with your auburn hair and green eyes.'

'Stop already with such silly ideas.' Gittel frowned over the sock. 'She'll noch want to be an actress. It's enough she reads all those books. Small wonder she talks in her sleep. At least if she'd speak in Yiddish I'd understand.'

Ruth smiled shyly at Berka over Gittel's head.

'The other night,' Gittel told the story for the tenth time, 'she got out of bed and put on her shoes. "Where are you going?" I asked her. "To school", our student replied. "To night school?" I asked.' Here Gittel smiled, pleased with her little joke. 'Go back to bed immediately,' I said and back to bed she went, grumbling. The day's not long enough for her. And where are you going now?' she asked as Ruth moved to the door.

'To Mavis. We're collecting silver paper from the streets and the veld. When we've made a big ball, we give it to the government to make bullets for the soldiers.'

'She's fighting the war single-handed,' Berka said. 'Clothing the soldiers, producing ammunition. Hitler won't last long with such an enemy.'

'I'd rather go to the Zionist meeting,' Ruth said wistfully. 'All the Jewish children go on Sunday mornings. They learn Hebrew songs and play games and get books to read. But Mommy won't let me go. She says there isn't money for uniforms and she doesn't like Zionists. Goodbye Zeide Berchik, I'll bring my silver paper ball to show you after school tomorrow.'

'Sweet child,' Berka said. 'You should see the walls in my workshop. Every inch of them is covered with her drawings. I still have the first one she did at school. Gittel, Sheinka should let her go to Zionist meetings. Ruth should mix with Jewish children.'

'Sheinka doesn't let her live,' Gittel said angrily. 'She must have someone to devour. With Dovid it doesn't work any more, so she takes it out on Ruth. And you should see the child hanging around her, waiting for a little love. Kadoches she gets.'

'Is she reconciled to the loss of Zutzke? She really loved that dog.'

'She still dreams about him,' Gittel said biting her lip. 'She wonders what she did that made Zutzke run away from her.'

She preferred not to think of Zutzke; she'd been an accomplice in his disappearance. One day she'd heard Sheinka speak to Avremala the poultry vender about taking Zutzke away. He's a danger to the health of my baby, she told him. His hairs give Phillip asthma. Avremala had shrugged, grabbed the squealing Zutzke by the scruff of his neck and stuffed him into an empty chicken cage. The squawks of the chickens and Zutzke's terrified yelps still rang in Gittel's ears. For weeks Ruthie had run through the streets looking for her dog. Berka, like everybody else, believed Zutzke had run away.

'Sheinka, I notice, isn't upset by the loss of Zutzke,' Berka said looking carefully at Gittel. 'Nachas from parents. Has it ever struck you Gittel, that we parents often get what we deserve? And it's not nachas I'm talking about.'

'Berka, what are you saying? I'm dropping my stitches. Eina links, eina rechts . . .' She manipulated the four needles with deft fingers, then folded up the knitting.

'Don't go,' Berka said. 'It's not often that I have an intelligent audience.'

'Teasing me again,' Gittel replied but she sat down. 'I remember when you had an intelligent audience. You and Hershl and Dovid used to sit out there on the veranda in summer and for hours the whole street would ring with your discussions. In those days the streets smelled of gefilte fish and tzimmes and other things. Now it smells of bacon. Those were the good years.'

'When we lived in the good old days, we were forever evoking other good old days.'

'You know what I mean. The children were young and we were all together . . .'

'I know what you mean, Gittel, and I've also had longings for the good old days. I miss, among other things, those talks on the veranda. Only Hershl had an inkling of what was happening. All Dovid wanted was to get back to the old country and make his revolution. But I was also wrong. Correction. I wasn't wrong; Hershl was right.'

'Berka, you've been marvellous just to survive all your troubles. I'd have been in a madhouse by now.'

'I don't know, Gittel. Things are changing too fast for me to keep up. I don't recognise the new Afrikaners. Just listen to what they're saying these days,' Berka said picking up the newspaper from the floor. "Hitler is not a barbarian. He is like Dr. Malan, who tries only to liberate his people . . . General Smuts is an imperialist who's making us fight England's wars . . . We and the Germans are the only true Aryans." And so on and so forth. I'm beginning to feel like a stranger in this terrifying new world.'

'Berka,' Gittel said getting up. 'Come over to our house sometimes. Dovid is as lonely as you. You can forgive him already.'

'We greet each other,' Berka said stiffly. 'Some things just, just die, I suppose.'

'Come anyway. I must go now. If I don't prepare lunch there won't be any. Sheinka's too busy with that spoilt brat of hers who's got the mumps.'

Ruth tiptoed into the house to fetch her silver paper ball. She did not want Sheinka to hear her. On the way out she peeped into the bedroom through the half-closed door. Phillip, whose swollen face was bandaged, was leaning against Sheinka as she paged through the photo album.

'And when you're bigger you'll also play the fiddle,' she was saying. 'I'll buy you a little black velvet suit and a white blouse with a round collar. You'll put the fiddle under your chin, just like this man in the picture, and you'll play the most beautiful sad songs. I only hope you'll have a better fate than he had, poor man. Such a woman . . .'

'I don't want a fiddle,' Phillip whimpered. 'It's sore under my chin. I want a motor car.'

A glass wall seemed to descend between them. Sheinka and Phillip drew further and further away until Ruth could barely hear them. The ache in her chest dissolved and was replaced by a frantic beating of her heart. As she stretched out her fingers, the glass wall receded. With her head spinning she turned away and went into her room.

She threw herself onto the bed and repeated feverishly: I am Ruth Erlich. I am Ruth Erlich. I go to Rand Mines Primary School and next year I'll be at High School. It's all right. It'll go away. This glass wall always melts away. Breathe slowly . . . Slowly . . . Think of ordinary things, of ordinary things . . .

Had she been a baby she would have called out to her father. But she was big now; her father didn't sing any more and her own throat closed up tightly as she was about to call him.

Think of ordinary things, she whispered urgently as she felt herself fading away again. If she went too far away she might never come back. Think, think. Tomorrow Daniel would walk to school with her again. He'd wait outside his gate, pretending to tie up his shoe laces or to look for something in his school bag. Then she'd come out of the house and he'd follow her to the veld and they'd walk together, silently often, but she knew he was her friend. You can play with our cats any time you like, he offered when Zutzke disappeared.

Zutzke, Zutzke. Where was he now? Starving in the veld? Dead? She used to fall asleep at night holding him close to her and the comfort of his warm, somewhat smelly body kept her nightmares away.

The pain in her chest started up again and the glass wall began to lift. She thrust her head into her pillow and cried bitterly.

Everything looked strange and distant as she walked out of the house, clutching her silver paper ball. She walked through the damp veld along the path that led to the school and to Mavis's house. It had rained the previous evening and the puddle was there again, as it had been on her first day of school. Raizel had jumped over it and said 'Mind the puddle!' Impatiently. One image followed another in rapid succession: Raizel fetching her from hospital after her tonsils operation; Raizel clutching her unbuttoned blouse in Dovid's workshop; Raizel standing behind Berka in the lounge, crying softly while her mother screamed on the sofa. That was the first time the glass wall had come down. She had been sitting on the floor with Zutzke, feeling frightened and somehow responsible for what was happening. Then suddenly they all seemed far away. She felt safe from them behind the glass wall.

Mavis was waiting for her impatiently outside her house.

'I thought you were never coming,' she said drawing Ruth away towards the veld. 'Let's go to our den. I've got so much to tell you. There's no time for collecting silver paper today.'

They walked over to a clump of blue gums whose enormous trunks had been partially destroyed by a veld fire. Mavis withheld her secret until they were seated on a fallen trunk.

'Thelma told me the secret. She's known it for a long time. When you're about thirteen you start to bleed. From your wee,' she said impatiently when Ruth looked puzzled. 'It's very sore. Sometimes it happens earlier, sometimes later,' she added knowledgeably.

Ruth turned pale and squeezed the silver paper ball tightly in her hand.

'But why? Why?'

'So's you can have babies of course,' Mavis said, surprised that Ruth did not see the connection. 'And Thelma said you mustn't let a boy touch you because you'd have a baby. Nor must you play with yourself, you know how.'

Ruth's heart beat uncomfortably. She panicked even when her nose bled.

'All the time? Does it bleed all the time?' she asked anxiously.

'No, silly. Only for a week a month. My mother's made bandages for Thelma and she has to wash them every day.'

She looked critically at Ruth's tiny breasts which were barely visible under her blouse. Then she touched her own rounded breasts proudly.

'You're not well enough developed to get your periods yet,' she said. 'That's what it's called. Periods. I'll start before you.'

Whom could she ask, Ruth wondered as she walked home. Who would explain? Gittel would say such things were not for the ears of young girls. Her mother would shout and make her feel ashamed. Raizel would have told her. She was the only one she might have turned to.

The sun shone fiercely out of a pale blue sky and the veld seemed grey and endless. The suburb, the mine dumps, the plantation and the dam looked still and distant, like a painting against a blue wall.

Ruth walked wearily over the veld and felt as though she was the only being on earth.

The following morning Ruth opened her eyes slowly, fearfully. Her grandmother's feather bed was still unmade, her school books lay scattered on the table where she had left them the previous evening and a soft breeze blew the curtains open, bringing in the smell of damp earth.

She closed her eyes and sighed with relief.

All was well. It had been a nightmare, a terrible nightmare. Her consciousness lapped around the edges of her dream, throwing up an image here and there, but the dream itself receded and left her with the bitter dregs. If only she could remember.

She lay back and listened to the sound of hushed voices from the kitchen. That was Chaya Schwartzman speaking. A stab of recognition went through her. Chaya had been in her dream. She must remember, she must remember.

She had lain in the hot dark room last night, unable to sleep. Now and again she heard the sound of distant thunder, then a wind blew up, parting the curtains and revealing a purple turbulent sky. An empty sky. God was not there for her any more. When she was small she had prayed to him through the gap in the curtains: Please stop my parents from fighting; let my mother love me; send away Phillip forever; let me find Zutzke. But the sky was as empty as Zeide Berchik's veld.

She could not fall asleep. Just once more, she promised herself, then I'll never do it again. She moved her hand slowly over her flat stomach, towards her rising breasts, then down again towards her thighs . . . Blood! Soon there would be blood spurting from there. She shuddered. After much tossing and turning she finally fell into a restless sleep.

As she did, there was a roar of planes in the sky. Bombs fell and flashes of fire lit up the dumps and dam. People streaked with blood ran screaming through the streets. She looked at the foot of her bed. Zutzke was gone. She had to find Zutzke. He'd be killed if she didn't find him. Her movements were slow and heavy; her need to find Zutzke urgent. She walked numbly out of the cluttered up room, into the dark passage, towards the front door. She lifted the latch and stepped onto the veranda.

Zutzke! She tried to call but no sound came from her throat. She watched the planes zoom into the distance and disappear but the sky still flashed with fire. The stones pricked her bare feet as she walked slowly, doggedly, towards Leib Schwartzman's house. She rang the bell once, twice, a third time. The lights went on in the passage and Chaya Schwartzman stood before her, clutching her night gown to her throat.

'Mrs. Blackman,' Ruth said then forgot what she had come about. Was it for the big black pot her grandmother wanted for taiglach? 'Mrs. Blackman,' she began again. 'There's been an air raid and I'm looking for Zutzke. He ran away from home. He could be killed.'

The voices from the kitchen, no longer hushed, could be heard clearly in her room.

'It's not so terrible Sheinka. Don't take on so. If it is a kind of madness, it's only temporary. It happened to Sora-Riva's daughter as well. She didn't walk, she used to sing in her sleep. Also at that age . . .'

Ruth began to cry softly. It had not been a dream. She remembered now. The veranda had felt wet and cold to her feet as she looked into the shocked faces of Chaya and Leib.

He put his jacket over her shoulders and led her gently back to her house. The pavement had been wet and muddy . . .

Ruth threw off her blankets and looked down at her feet. They were caked with mud. The sheets were dirty. Stiff with horror she listened to the conversation from the kitchen.

'I'm to blame.' Sheinka was crying. 'I should never have taken the dog away from her.'

'Don't blame yourself. It's not the dog,' Chaya comforted her. 'I'm telling you. Some girls take it harder than others. Once she starts menstruating she'll become normal again. The blood boils and flows wildly through the body until it's time to break out. And of course, when the moon is full you must shut all the curtains. That brings on the walking. And put a bowl of cold water at the foot of her bed . . .'

'I'm mad, I'm mad!' Ruth bit into her pillow to stop herself from screaming. 'I'll never be like other girls. God! Why did you let me born?'

17

*D*ovid stood under the recently installed, sole neon sign in Mayfontein which flashed out: 'Sharp's (Pty) Ltd., Confectioners of Distinction.' It was Saturday morning and the shop was crowded. He weighed up the possibility of passing through unnoticed towards the back exit which led to the new bakery. The chances were slim, he decided. At the counter nearest the door Sora-Riva Sher was slicing brisket under a rail of polonies, sausage and smoked meat.

'Honestly,' her customer complained loudly. 'It's months since I've seen a piece of Scotch salmon. There's a war on, like everybody says, but the snoek is coming out of my ears already. And they say that for money you can buy anything.'

Dovid gagged and moved away from the door. He would take the long way around to the offices. As he passed Leib's old smithy he recalled Hershl's plans for converting it into a tea room. He had given up the idea when he built the bakery. Dovid glanced across at Berka's workshop before he turned into Lover's Lane. The last stood idle and Berka sat at his bench, reading a newspaper. He looked up, caught Dovid's eye, nodded, then turned back to his paper. It was the first time they had seen one another since Dovid moved out of Mayfontein eight months ago. He had not wanted to move but Ruth was miserable after the news of her sleepwalk had spread through the suburb. The children teased her, the adults treated her like an idiot child. Yenta lent them money — I'm doing it for my sister Gittel, she told Dovid when he demurred — and they moved over the hills into an orange brick suburb. Ruth, at least, was happy now.

Dovid turned into Lover's Lane, then into a large asphalt square at the back of Sharp's which divided the shop from the two-storey building that housed the bakery and the offices. Six large vans were parked outside a section marked 'Despatch' and teams of black men were packing bread into the shelving of the vans.

> Like animals they were herded into vans, tightly packed so that they could hardly breathe. Not that it mattered; they would not breathe for long anyway. Children cried, mothers panicked and the frightened men prayed. To whom? They arrived at their destination blue-lipped, soiled, dead.

Dovid's palms sweated and his breathing came in heavy, uneven gasps. He must take a hold on himself, present a calm, sane front to Hershl. He stood in the middle of the square and watched some black men unload a miller's truck piled high with bags of flour. Two of them lowered a heavy bag onto the back of a third. With a heave and a grunt the men walked slowly up a ramp into the bakery's store. As he went by Dovid saw that his face was powdered with flour. It clung to his short curly eyelashes and eyebrows, emphasising features not readily seen on a black face. Dovid suppressed a surge of hysterical laughter which bubbled up to his throat.

'Are you looking for someone, Mr. Erlich?' a polite voice asked at his side. It was Dirk Venter, the chief baker. Dovid swallowed painfully and said:

'Hello Dirk. I've come to see Mr. Singer, but I can't find my way around.'

'I'll take you to the lift,' Dirk offered. 'It's difficult to find if you don't know the place. You see, the ground floor holds the stores and the despatch and the bread ovens . . .'

Ovens . . .

'. . . and on the first floor is the confectionery. Are you not well, Mr. Erlich? You've suddenly gone so white. Here, sit down while we wait for the lift. You'll find the offices on the second floor. Things have changed, eh? Do you remember those tiny wall ovens in the shop next door to Chidrawi? I worked alone then, with only Mr. and Mrs. Singer and a few kaffirs. Do you remember, Mr. Erlich?'

'I remember.' Dovid forced a smile as he stepped into the lift.

> Berka and Hershl laughing in the doorway,
> Raizel cashing up. Go home Berka. I want to
> speak to Raizel. Something important to say but
> forgotten what. Lost, lost. In the vans, in the
> veld . . .

'Whom do you want to see?' The telephonist looked suspiciously at Dovid. 'Mr. Singer? He's busy. Do you have an appointment?'

She rang through to Hershl's office and announced with disapproval:

'A Mr. Erlich to see you. He hasn't got an appointment. Yes, Mr. Singer, yes, Mr. Singer.'

'Sit down please,' she said grudgingly. 'Mr. Singer will see you soon. He has someone in with him at the moment.'

Dovid took the morning paper from a little table. It was some time before it made sense to him. Then he smiled. World-shaking events: A Nationalist meeting at the nerve-centre of the universe, Ermelo. Mr. Pirow of the New Order and Dr. Verwoerd of the Herenigde party had spoken from the same platform. Pirow wanted National Socialism in South Africa but an Afrikaner version, not the German kind. Political systems did not transplant readily; look at democracy in South Africa. Verwoerd differed from him on one point: He disliked the name National Socialism. Fastidious man. Dovid threw the paper back onto the table.

A fussy little man with a file under his arm walked towards the lift.

'Go in now,' the telephonist said to Dovid in a tone that indicated she'd have preferred him not to. 'First office on the right.'

A long row of offices stretched down the corridor. 'Accountant', 'Invoicing', 'Typists', Dovid read. And on the frosted upper half of the first office on the right he saw 'Harry M. Singer, Director'. He hesitated, looked towards the lift, then knocked.

'Come in, Dovidke, come in. Since when do you knock on my door?'

Dovid walked in. Hershl sat behind an enormous glass-topped desk piled with papers and files. He was dressed in a dark suit which Dovid had made him last Rosh Hashana. He's put on weight, Dovid noted: three inches to be let out of the waist. His balding head shone and his double chin spread around his face as he smiled up genially at Dovid.

'Why do I knock?' Dovid asked. 'What else does one do before a gilded name plate? The Harry I understand, an English translation of Hershl, I suppose. But the 'M'? What does that stand for? Money? Or were you on the point of death that they added a name for you in shul?'

'Dovid!' Hershl's face crumbled in dismay. 'What is it? Why are you so, so, bitter? So strange? I hardly recognise you. It's not a terrible thing to change a name, to add a name. To my friends I'll always be Hershl Singer. In business one plays their game.'

Dovid sat down in the leather armchair and passed a hand wearily over his eyes.

'Forgive me, Hershl. I've not been myself lately. I think I'm going mad.'

Dovid's skin was drawn tightly over his cheekbones and a vein beat rapidly at his temple. His eyes, as he lifted them to Hershl, glittered unnaturally from their sunken sockets and were full of pain. Not so long ago, Hershl thought sadly, Dovid was talking about a golden age in Lithuania. His hair had faded to a powdered auburn and lay damply against his creased forehead. He slumped in the chair and rubbed his right hand nervously with his left.

'What is it, Dovid?' he asked gently. 'You look as though you've peered into the blackest pits of hell.'

'Haven't you?' Dovid began aggressively. 'Or are you insulated from misery by wealth? Money, they say, can buy anything, even peace of mind. Certainly an easy conscience.'

'Dovid, how can you say that to me?'

'So you give employment to the poor and the crippled and the old. And you give money to charity and your Zionist cause. Does that help the doomed Jews in Europe?'

Hershl did not reply. He looked down at the papers on his desk and sighed.

'One does only what one can.'

'I'm sorry, Hershl. Words pour out of me before I can stop them. But how can one breathe, live, eat, when the civilised world is collapsing about our heads? I lie awake at night and wonder which fate has befallen my family. Were they among those who were shot before open graves, the dead buried with the dying? Or were they among those herded into synagogues, starved, then burned alive? Or are they languishing in concentration camps? I hear nothing but the screams of dying people; I smell nothing but smoke and scorched flesh, and when I shut my eyes the nightmares begin. And I do nothing about it. How much can the flesh endure before it disintegrates in agony?'

Dovid covered his face with his hands. Sobs shuddered through his emaciated body. Hershl squeezed his eyes tightly together and dug his nails deeply into the flesh of his palms.

'Dovid, Dovid . . .'

'Help me,' Dovid turned his tortured eyes onto Hershl. 'Help me at least to dispel the uncertainty, to complete my nightmare. I must know what happened to my family. You know people in high places. Ask them to find out what happened to the people of Ragaza.'

'We've tried, Dovid. I have two brothers and a sister in Vilna. Faigel's whole family is there, was there, who knows these days? Last week Yaakov Koren came in to enquire about his wife and children. We've traced no one. All we know is that Ragaza was occupied by the Nazis and that the notorious pogromist Zappenpfennig has been appointed Governor of Vilna.'

'Ask the Red Cross. They find people.'

'We have. They can't help us. Foreign embassies don't know. We've been in touch with organisations in Switzerland, but nobody's been able to pierce the black cloud over Nazi-occupied Europe. We've got to be strong, Dovid, and learn to live in uncertainty, in helplessness and to do only what we can. Take heart. The war's taken a turn for the better. With the Americans in, it will be over soon . . .'

'When they're dead, when they're all dead!' Dovid cried. 'Hershl, my life is tied up with theirs. I should have been there, suffering with them, dying with them. What am I doing here, a stranger, a deserter? When they were alive I hardly wrote, didn't send money, but I belong with them. Their fate should be mine.'

'Don't lose hope, Dovid. The Russians have evacuated civilians into the interior. Perhaps your family is among them.'

'They're all my family; the ones who are trapped in the Warsaw Ghetto, the Lithuanians, the Russians, the Poles. And they wouldn't take me into the army. On the South African fascists I broke my hand while the Nazis slaughter my people in Europe.'

'There's little we can do except harass powerful statesmen, hope and pray. The Americans worry about what Congress will say; Britain is afraid to offend the Arabs. So that even those who might still be saved are left to their bitter fate. Dovid, I feel as helpless as you.'

They were both silent for a while. Why had he come to see Hershl? He could tell him nothing new. Dovid had been haunting the offices of Jewish organisations for months. He hardly worked and his hand ached unbearably at times. After he had closed down his workshop in Mayfontein, he did alterations and sewed trousers for other tailors, barely earning enough to keep his family clothed and fed. He had finally become a haizenschneider, a trousermaker.

'. . . and give up your tailoring,' Hershl was saying.

'What? I, I was, my mind was wandering. I didn't hear you, Hershl.'

'I said you should give up tailoring. Come and work for me.'

Dovid laughed.

'Thank you. Another social case, another cripple on your staff. I don't want your charity.'

'I'm not offering charity Dovid. I need you. It's impossible to get honest reliable men these days. And I'd like to work with you. One gets so cut off from people one really cares about.'

'You don't need me. You're a successful man, with a well-organised business. You can get anyone you need without encumbering your staff with yet another misfit.'

'So you think I'm such a success? In a way I suppose I am, but I don't measure happiness in gold. All I ever wanted was money enough to emigrate to Palestine. I've never been further from my dreams than I am now.'

'Dreams? Who dreams? It's all a nightmare.'

'Dovid, you don't have to give me an answer now. Think about it. It's a quiet job I'm offering you, away from the crowds in the shop. You'd be the storeman for the shop, in Leib's old smithy. I'm telling you the truth. I need you more than you need me . . . Yenta!' he cried as she burst into the office, pale and agitated. She had both hands over her breast and was quite breathless.

'It's Yaakov . . . Koren, unfortunate man. He's thrown himself into the dam. They're there now, dredging it, looking for his body. Widow Kagan's screaming, crying. He left a note. "I killed my wife and children. I go to join them." That's all. Hershl, who can plumb the depths of human suffering? Such guilts he must have had. And he wasn't sure that his wife and children were dead.'

'They're dead,' Dovid said woodenly, getting out of the chair. 'Grodno was razed to the ground by the Nazis.'

'Foolish tortured man,' Hershl said bitterly. 'Another victory for Hitler. Another Jew dead. But who can judge?'

'Goodbye,' Dovid said softly and walked out of the office with a stoney expression on his face.

'Stop him, Hershl,' Yenta pleaded. 'God alone knows what he'll do.'

'Leave him Yenta. Every man is responsible for his own fate.'

'I shouldn't have burst in like that. Such ideas Dovid doesn't need. Gittel says he's off his head as it is. He won't touch meat, says there's a smell of burning flesh everywhere. Throws windows open as soon as he gets into the house. He doesn't sleep and he doesn't work. He just runs around from office to office trying to trace his family. He'll land up like Koren.'

'He might have,' Hershl reflected, 'but he's got too much pride to follow a mere trousermaker to the grave. Yentala, the heart's stronger than iron if it doesn't burst from pain and from helplessness.'

Hitler's march on Moscow stemmed, Berka read. But Smolensk lies devastated, he thought wearily, and Kiev had fallen. Chmielnicki's hordes have risen again with perfected means for death and torture.

He looked up from his newspaper into the haunted eyes of Dovid. Like a spectre from the grave. Berka nodded, then turned away his eyes from the thin, pitiable figure on the corner of Lover's Lane.

Enough work. Berka looked with wry amusement at the untouched shoe on his last: Mrs. Melamed could wait until Monday. Now for the real work of the day, the walk up Main Street hill. Every year it grew steeper.

He folded up the newspaper and left it on the workbench. It was good only for wrapping up old shoes. He no longer charted the course of the war. His map hung untouched on the wall between the yellowed patches where Yenta's relatives had simpered and smirked in sepia.

He should hang Ruthie's drawings up in the lounge and cover up the ghosts of the past, he thought as he walked around the shop slowly, stopping now and then before a dog-eared drawing. Here was one of him on an ox wagon with Zutzke, kindly lent for company. She had captured the feeling of desolation so well. Loneliness is grey, she had said. Even his moustache drooped wearily. And here was a picture of people huddled under a tree while a plane spat fire from the sky.

'Words', she had said gravely when he asked after her first day at school what she most wanted to learn. Her drawings were more eloquent than any words she would ever learn. Poor child. His heart ached when he thought of the toil, hope and disillusion that still lay ahead of her.

He walked out of his shop and took a deep breath. Spring. The first rains had washed the mine dust from the air and through the smell of damp concrete, exhaust and Hershl's fresh bread, he thought he smelled blossoms. By now the veld fires had charred the grass to black stubble, the farmer had taken to his plough and a new cycle would begin.

Perhaps on the land life had retained some meaning. Or perhaps there too it was reduced to the monotonous cycle of birth, growth, death and rebirth. It wearied him to think of it.

There was definitely a smell of blossoms in the air. Berka drew in another deep breath and his lungs caught on the smell of exhaust. Spring. It was a season for lovers, farmers and warlords. For old men it was a mockery.

He looked beyond the Dip towards the city and mourned for its transience. A few bombs and it would suffer the fate of older, nobler cities. Like a proud fortress it towered over the suburb at its gates and he had never suspected its vulnerability.

Yet life went on. He viewed it with detachment, surprised at his former involvement and passion. Along the same arteries flowed the old with the new: the miners' wives he had pitied; the black men whose lot he had lamented; the hungry children he longed to feed, and the shoppers who arrived in their shiny cars from other suburbs.

There would always be poverty and oppression alongside of wealth and greed, whether he hammered away at his last all day or whether he sat back to read the chronicle of daily disasters.

He walked slowly up Main Street, stopping for breath only when a jagged pain pierced his chest. Tolerance, he thought. It was a word whose meaning he had forgotten. For him the line between tolerance and indifference had become smudged. In the shadow of death one became obsessed with one's mortality. Not that he was afraid of dying. It was a process which one experienced throughout one's life. If a man could live in isolation, without emotional bonds, without love or hate, he might live forever. As it was, his life was tied up with that of others and was diminished by each death, withdrawal or rejection.

But when he looked into the dark interior of Nathan's Drapery Store, he was surprised to find that the shell of his

171

being still ached with longing and nostalgia.

It was some time before he sensed the excitement in Main Street. Everybody seemed to be hurrying in the direction of the mine dumps.

'What is it?' he asked a group of miners who stood outside the bar, talking earnestly among themselves.

'That crazy Bolshie Koren drowned himself,' one of them replied. 'Just walked into the dam and disappeared into the slime. They're looking for his body.'

Berka walked past First Avenue towards the plantation. People were converging on the dam from all directions. He paused at the top of the hill and looked about him. The mine dumps shimmered palely in the warm spring sun and the bluegums hung sadly over the dam. In the distance the headgear turned ceaselessly and the roar of the crushers reverberated throughout the suburb.

'My kingdom,' he thought grimly, and breathing heavily, made his way down to the dam.

Safe Houses

Rose Zwi

1993 Top Twenty Title, Listener Women's Book Festival

In *Safe Houses*, three families—black and Jewish—are inextricably bound by love and hate, hope and treachery. Linked by a common past, separated by betrayal, Ruth and Lola are drawn into the struggle against apartheid.

Safe Houses is the story of a unique friendship that develops against all the odds and reveals the complexities of apartheid and racial discrimination.

Rose Zwi was born in Mexico, but spent most of her life in South Africa. Her previous novels include *The Umbrella Tree, Another Year in Africa, The Inverted Pyramid* and *Exiles*. She has won several prizes for her work in South Africa. In 1988 Rose emigrated to Australia and now lives in Sydney.

"The story encompasses the perspectives of black and white characters, real people coming to terms with personal and political change. Against a background of township violence, fear and prejudice, the author deals with issues of race, cultural appropriation, youth and age, and both petty and powerful politics."

– Faith Bandler

"Zwi has set out to capture the full sweep of events during this difficult period and her novel is a remarkable achievement."

– Leon Trainer, *Australian*

Fiction   1-875559-21-3 $18.95   200 pages   198 x 128
Territory: World   All rights: Spinifex

The Falling Woman

Susan Hawthorne

1992 Top Twenty Title, Listener Women's Book Festival

The Falling Woman memorably dramatises a desert journey in which two women confront ancient and modern myths, ranging from the Garden of Eden to the mystique of epilepsy, and the mysteries of the universe itself. In the guise of three personae, the falling woman struggles to find the map for her life and meet the challenge of her own survival.

Susan Hawthorne is the author of *The Spinifex Quiz Book* as well as the editor of five anthologies including *Angels of Power*. Her collection of poems, *The Language in My Tongue*, was published in the volume *Four New Poets*. Her work has been widely published internationally. She lives in Melbourne.

"A remarkable, lyrical first novel that weaves together such disparate themes as the mystery of epilepsy, love between women, and an odyssey across the Australian desert."

– Ms Magazine

"Hawthorne shows assurance, a powerful historical and cultural imagination and a rich feel for language."

– John Hanrahan, Age

Fiction   1-875559-04-3 $17.95   288 pages   198 x 128
Territory: World   All rights: Spinifex

Zelda

Zelda D'Aprano

*An autobiography that describes the way Australian lives
and women's lives have changed over the last 60 years.*

Zelda is the life story of the extraordinary Zelda D'Aprano, born
in Melbourne of Jewish working-class parents. She chained herself to the Arbitration Building in Melbourne in the late 60s, in
protest against unequal wages; refused to pay any more than 75
per cent of the full tram fare since women's wages were 75 per
cent of men's; was one of four women to call a meeting in a
Melbourne living room which signalled the beginning of the
women's movement.

Zelda's life was a constant battle against poverty, ignorance
and discrimination. She sought to understand oppression and
injustice and to fight against it. A book full of drama and working-
class humour, *Zelda* is the story of D'Aprano's experience in the
work-force, trade unions and left wing politics, and how she
began to analyse these structures and eventually question the
relevance of male politics to the lives and needs of women. An
Afterword outlines the shift in the women's movement over the
past 20 years.

"*Zelda* is a document of the 1970s, but it is also a book for our
times . . . and contributes importantly to debate today."

– Marilyn Lake, *Age*

"Zelda's story is essential reading for anyone seeking a better
understanding of the struggle for women's rights in this
country."   – Julia Hancock, *LOTL*

*Non-fiction/autobiography   1-875559-30-2 $19.95   415 pages
198 x 128   Territory: World   All rights: Spinifex*

Tansie

Erika Kimpton

Alix Clemenger, sophisticate and internationally famous composer and concert pianist, is the toast of high society. A succession of momentous milestones has determined her life and career, the last is when she meets Tansie Landon. Tansie, beautiful, enigmatic, fragile, is—although not yet successful—an exceptional sculptor. But Tansie's childhood of abuse and neglect has left her so emotionally scarred that love has become a source of embattlement.

When Tansie begins to display towards Alix the same harshness and indifference she knew as a child, she tests Alix's love to its limit and pushes herself to the edge of destruction. In the end Tansie's gift to Alix is a lesson in the possibilities and limitations of love.

Erika Kimpton was born and raised in Switzerland where she studied Interior Architecture before she came to Australia in 1967. Since then she has enjoyed a successful career as an interior designer before taking to writing fiction. This is her first novel. She continues to work in her profession, travels extensively and is currently working on her second and third novels. She lives in Melbourne with her four children.

Fiction   1-875559-34-5 $16.95   413 pages   198 x 129
Territory: World   All Rights: Spinifex

Figments of a Murder
Gillian Hanscombe

An extraordinary novel about revenge and its repercussions by Gillian Hanscombe, a writer who combines lyricism, intellect and irreverence in this whodunnit of revenge amongst women.

Babes is the toast of London's women's community – always there, always right, always surrounded by her favourites. But Babes was not everyone's favourite. Indeed, for Tessa, "Babes is the worst of women." With an array of characters including Gloriana Hardy, the writer who has made it, Sybil—a ventriloquist doll—and her companion Tessa, Sarah and Ashok, who cook and think but never argue, and Riva the therapist, Gillian Hanscombe weaves an intricate web of intrigue.

Gillian Hanscombe is the author of three collections of poetry, *Hecate's Charms*, *Flesh and Paper* (with Suniti Namjoshi), and *Sybil: The Glide of Her Tongue*, as well as works of fiction and non-fiction. She currently lives in Devon, UK.

Novel   1-875559-43-4 $16.95   264 pages   198 x 128
Territory: World   All Rights: Spinifex